Muslims in America

OTHER BOOKS OF RELATED INTEREST

OPPOSING VIEWPOINTS SERIES
Civil Liberties
Extremist Groups
Hate Groups
Human Rights
Immigration
Iraq
Islam
National Security
Religion in America
The War on Terrorism

CURRENT CONTROVERSIES SERIES
Civil Liberties
Homeland Security
Iraq
The Middle East
Racism
The Terrorist Attack on America

AT ISSUE SERIES
The Attack on America: September 11, 2001
Homeland Security
Islamic Fundamentalism
Is Racism a Serious Problem?
Media Bias
National Security

Muslims in America

Allen Verbrugge, *Book Editor*

Bruce Glassman, *Vice President*
Bonnie Szumski, *Publisher*
Helen Cothran, *Managing Editor*
David M. Haugen, *Series Editor*

Contemporary Issues Companion

GREENHAVEN PRESS
An imprint of Thomson Gale, a part of The Thomson Corporation

THOMSON
GALE

Detroit • New York • San Francisco • San Diego • New Haven, Conn.
Waterville, Maine • London • Munich

THOMSON
_____★_____™
GALE

The Chicago Public Library
Garfield Ridge Branch
6348 S. Archer Avenue
Chicago Il. 60638
312-747-6094

LIBRARY OF CONGRESS CATALOGING-IN-PUBLICATION DATA

Muslims in America / Allen Verbrugge, book editor.
    p. cm. — (Contemporary issues companion)
Includes bibliographical references and index.
ISBN 0-7377-2315-7 (lib. : alk. paper) — ISBN 0-7377-2316-5 (pbk. : alk. paper)
    1. Muslims—United States—Social conditions. 2. United States—Ethnic relations. I. Verbrugge, Allen. II. Series.
E184.M88M86 2005
305.6'97'0973—dc22   2004050096

Printed in the United States of America

CONTENTS

FOREWORD

In the news, on the streets, and in neighborhoods, individuals are confronted with a variety of social problems. Such problems may affect people directly: A young woman may struggle with depression, suspect a friend of having bulimia, or watch a loved one battle cancer. And even the issues that do not directly affect her private life—such as religious cults, domestic violence, or legalized gambling—still impact the larger society in which she lives. Discovering and analyzing the complexities of issues that encompass communal and societal realms as well as the world of personal experience is a valuable educational goal in the modern world.

Effectively addressing social problems requires familiarity with a constantly changing stream of data. Becoming well informed about today's controversies is an intricate process that often involves reading myriad primary and secondary sources, analyzing political debates, weighing various experts' opinions—even listening to first-hand accounts of those directly affected by the issue. For students and general observers, this can be a daunting task because of the sheer volume of information available in books, periodicals, on the evening news, and on the Internet. Researching the consequences of legalized gambling, for example, might entail sifting through congressional testimony on gambling's societal effects, examining private studies on Indian gaming, perusing numerous websites devoted to Internet betting, and reading essays written by lottery winners as well as interviews with recovering compulsive gamblers. Obtaining valuable information can be time-consuming—since it often requires researchers to pore over numerous documents and commentaries before discovering a source relevant to their particular investigation.

Greenhaven's Contemporary Issues Companion series seeks to assist this process of research by providing readers with useful and pertinent information about today's complex issues. Each volume in this anthology series focuses on a topic of current interest, presenting informative and thought-provoking selections written from a wide variety of viewpoints. The readings selected by the editors include such diverse sources as personal accounts and case studies, pertinent factual and statistical articles, and relevant commentaries and overviews. This diversity of sources and views, found in every Contemporary Issues Companion, offers readers a broad perspective in one convenient volume.

In addition, each title in the Contemporary Issues Companion series is designed especially for young adults. The selections included in every volume are chosen for their accessibility and are expertly edited in consideration of both the reading and comprehension levels of the audience. The structure of the anthologies also enhances accessibility. An introductory essay places each issue in context and provides helpful facts such as historical background or current statistics and legislation that pertain to the topic. The chapters that follow organize the material and focus on specific aspects of the book's topic. Every essay is introduced by a brief summary of its main points and biographical information about the author. These summaries aid in comprehension and can also serve to direct readers to material of immediate interest and need. Finally, a comprehensive index allows readers to efficiently scan and locate content.

The Contemporary Issues Companion series is an ideal launching point for research on a particular topic. Each anthology in the series is composed of readings taken from an extensive gamut of resources, including periodicals, newspapers, books, government documents, the publications of private and public organizations, and Internet websites. In these volumes, readers will find factual support suitable for use in reports, debates, speeches, and research papers. The anthologies also facilitate further research, featuring a book and periodical bibliography and a list of organizations to contact for additional information.

A perfect resource for both students and the general reader, Greenhaven's Contemporary Issues Companion series is sure to be a valued source of current, readable information on social problems that interest young adults. It is the editors' hope that readers will find the Contemporary Issues Companion series useful as a starting point to formulate their own opinions about and answers to the complex issues of the present day.

INTRODUCTION

On Tuesday, September 11, 2001, four U.S. passenger airplanes on domestic routes were hijacked and deliberately piloted into terrible crashes. Two planes hit the World Trade Center skyscrapers in New York City, causing those landmarks to collapse into rubble; another plane slammed into the western wing of the Pentagon building in Washington, D.C.; the fourth plane went down in a remote field in Pennsylvania. Nearly three thousand people lost their lives. Last-minute cell phone dispatches from doomed passengers provided information about the identities of the perpetrators—they appeared to be Arabic terrorists. As more information surfaced, the horror of the events of September 11 was traced to agents of the Islamic fundamentalist terrorist group al Qaeda.

The entire nation, and much of the world, was overwhelmed by the tragedy of that day. The anxieties of the moment were compounded for the 3 to 7 million Muslims living in America, who saw their worst nightmares realized. The identification of the hijackers gave further ammunition to those who would fear and scorn all Muslims because of the persistent stereotype of Muslims as extremists and terrorists.

In the aftermath of the September 11 attacks, Muslims in America had reason to fear for their personal safety, their public image, and their political agenda. While this minority group faced the possibility of becoming even more marginalized, Muslims in America turned some of the initial backlash into opportunity for greater outreach and a stronger, more united community.

Threats Against Muslims Post–September 11

Incidents of harassment and sometimes violence against Muslims in America were reported almost immediately after September 11. Despite the actions of Muslim American leaders and advocacy groups, who promptly and unanimously denounced actions of terrorism as aberrant to their religion, Muslims and even non-Muslim Americans of Arab descent became objects of suspicion, fear, or hatred. Within two weeks of the attack, at least five Middle Eastern students had been assaulted on college campuses, and several others had received threats. According to FBI reports, the vast majority of hate crimes in 2001 that targeted mosques, Islamic centers, and Arab American–owned businesses occurred in the three weeks after the attack. The American-Arab Anti-Discrimination Committee, which typically fielded about two hundred complaints of harassment each year, addressed over one hundred such complaints in only six weeks immediately following the September 11 attacks. "We have had a feeling of fear and wondering what will happen. People feel they are going to be singled out," said Imad Hamad, regional Midwest director of the committee. "They've been asking, 'Are we going to see massive arrests? Are we going to be the subject of hate crimes?'"

But these anti-Muslim actions were the exception, and the better nature of most Americans could be seen in the days and weeks following the tragedies. Americans of all faiths stood together in vigil and moved together to help through volunteer efforts and charitable donations. President George W. Bush made public statements in support of the American Muslim community and cautioned Americans against associating Islam, an international religion of peace, with the actions of a few madmen. Americans responded positively by volunteering to stand guard at mosques to help protect them against vandalism or by walking Muslim children to school to ensure their safety. And America's Muslims took note: Muqtedar Khan of the Center for the Study of Islam and Democracy wrote,

> In many places hundreds of Americans have gathered around Islamic centers in symbolic gestures of protection and embrace of American Muslims. In many cities Christian congregations have started wearing *hijab* [a veil worn by Muslim women] to identify with fellow Muslim women. In patience and in tolerance ordinary Americans have demonstrated their extraordinary virtues.

Although the majority of Americans came to support the American Muslim community, isolated incidents of bias against Muslims do occur. A report released by the Council on American-Islamic Relations (CAIR), a prominent national Islamic civil rights and advocacy group, outlined 1,019 incidents of anti-Muslim violence, discrimination, and harassment in 2003, the highest number of Muslim civil rights cases recorded since 1995, when the group began recording such statistics. Factors contributing to this trend, according to CAIR, include prowar rhetoric related to U.S. military efforts in Afghanistan and Iraq, a lingering atmosphere of fear and mistrust post–September 11, and an increase in anti-Muslim rhetoric on radio talk shows.

Muslims in the Public Eye

As the American public grappled with the fact that Muslim extremists had attacked their country, they began to learn more about the religion of Islam and the Muslims living in their midst. Islamic societies and culture, and specifically those Muslims living in America, sparked interest and curiosity. Leaders of American Muslim groups appeared frequently on news programs, and the public readily consumed information about Islam in books and magazine articles.

This new interest in Islam belied the fact that the Muslim American community has long been a part of the nation's tapestry and that in many ways its experiences are not at all atypical of any other ethnic or religious immigrant group. Muslims first immigrated to America in numbers in the late nineteenth century, and they have since become the nation's largest religious minority. Government data puts the number of mosques in the United States at more than twelve hundred; mosques can be found in each of the fifty states, from New York to Iowa, Alaska to Texas. Since immigrating, Muslims have experienced misunderstanding and discrimination, like any other religious or ethnic minority group. And like any other such group, Muslims have learned to adapt to the United States and have striven to bring their customs, traditions, and religious laws into accord with the ethos of their homeland.

Even though the country's attention to its Muslim citizens may have been borne out of a post–September 11 fear or suspicion, Muslims were able to leverage the increased attention into positive outreach. Riad Abdelkarim of the Council on American-Islamic Relations described what he felt were lessons learned by Muslims after the fateful day:

> Finally, Muslims began to reach out to their neighbors and to other faith and ethnic groups. Mosques and Islamic centers around the country began to hold open houses for their non-Muslim neighbors. Muslims have participated in earnest in interfaith gatherings and in town hall meetings with local, state and federal government officials.

Muslim Political Activism Post–September 11

Prior to September 11, Muslims in America were only beginning to find a political voice. While organizations like the Council on American-Islamic Relations and the Muslim Public Affairs Council were in place for some political lobbying, many Muslims, especially recent immigrants, were ambiguous about participation in the American political system; some Islamic groups maintained that American Muslims should focus on practicing and disseminating Islam and that participating in politics would be akin to accepting a corrupt society. Muslim leaders had never even made a unified endorsement of a presidential candidate until the 2000 elections.

The events of September 11 dissolved whatever political agenda may have existed for Muslims in America up to that point. Where they had been proactively advocating issues important to American Muslims, Muslim groups were immediately put on the defensive, and any political capital their burgeoning efforts may have established was instantly weakened.

Paradoxically, the defensive position in which Muslim American political groups found themselves in the aftermath of September 11 created a greater unity among these groups than had previously existed. The defensive position gave Muslims the opportunity to take stock of their numbers and resources and the impetus to exercise more political influence going forward.

By September 2003, when thousands gathered in Chicago for the Islamic Society of North America meeting, Agha Saeed of the Muslim American Congress was able to lead an excited crowd in a chant: "I am an American, I am a Muslim, and I vote," he said. National Muslim leaders announced plans to register 1 million Muslim voters in time for the 2004 presidential elections. Among those sources of new Muslim voters are young Muslims who make up a large proportion of the whole population. To reach them, an organization called the Muslim Electorate Council has run an Internet voter registration campaign, signing up some fifty-eight hundred voters in six months.

Sentiment regarding Muslim participation in politics has undergone a sea change. A 2003 study conducted by University of Kentucky political scientist for the Institute of Social Policy and Understanding found that 93 percent of mosque-attending Muslims agreed that American Muslims should be involved in politics. Even among the most religiously conservative Muslims, two-thirds supported active participation in U.S. politics. This finding demonstrates that the Muslim community "is clearly not willing to isolate itself from American society," the study found. Now more united than ever, the Muslim American constituency has established itself as a coveted political lobby, and the voices of Muslims are being heard on issues from U.S. foreign policy in the Middle East to domestic issues of concern, such as civil rights, racial profiling, hate crimes legislation, and faith-based public services initiatives. The current Muslim political establishment may owe much of its cohesiveness to the tragic crisis of the September 11 attacks.

September 11, 2001, was a watershed moment in contemporary American history. It tragically affected all Americans and certainly impacted the lives of Muslims in America. That there were some encouraging aftereffects for Muslims in America suggests that this community may heal and gain strength and that these gains may be part of the legacy of that tragic day.

CHAPTER 1

A HISTORY OF ISLAM AND MUSLIMS IN AMERICA

Contemporary Issues
Companion

ISLAM: ITS ORIGINS AND PRACTICE

Richard Wormser

Perhaps the most important factor in understanding the experiences of Muslims in America is a greater knowledge of the religion of Islam itself. In this selection from his book *American Islam: Growing Up Muslim in America*, Richard Wormser provides a brief overview of the life of the prophet Muhammad, the birth of Islam in the seventh century A.D., and the teachings of the Koran. In addition, he explains the five fundamental tenets of the faith, the primary holy days, and the basic differences between the Sunni and Shiite branches of Islam. To put these ancient Islamic traditions in a modern and personal context, Wormser illustrates his explanations with comments from young American Muslims, some of whom requested that only their first names be given. Wormser is a reporter, author, and filmmaker based in New York City.

"No one," says Ahmad Hassan, an Egyptian student, "can understand what Islam means to us without having some understanding of what we believe and the importance of the prophet Muhammad in our lives. Yet, despite the differences, there are many points of contact between us and Judaism and Christianity. There's a lot of things we share which could unite us rather than separate us."

Islam—like Judaism and Christianity—was born in the harsh, desert lands of the Middle East. In Egypt, Moses led the Jewish people out of bondage. In Nazareth, Jesus Christ was born, and in Jerusalem, he was crucified. Near Mecca, in the Arabian peninsula, the prophet Muhammad gave the Arabian people Islam. These three holy men—who had much in common—founded the faiths and ideals that almost two billion people believe today.

The Life of Muhammad

Muhammad was born to a poor family around the year A.D. 570 in the town of Mecca. Mecca was then famous as a trading center and for its many religious shrines that the Arabian tribes held sacred. When Muhammad was a child, his parents died and he was adopted by an uncle, Abu Talib. As a young man, Muhammad worked for a rich widow named Khadija, whom he eventually married.

One day, in about A.D. 610, Muhammad had a dream while in a mountain cave. In the dream, the angel Gabriel (called Jibril in Arabic) appeared and revealed to Muhammad words that were to become the first words of the Quran, the holy book of Muslims which they believe contains the revealed word of God. Shortly after the dream, Muhammad heard a voice say to him, "You are a messenger of God!" "I was standing," Muhammad was reported to have said, "but I fell on my knees and dragged myself along while the upper part of my chest was trembling." Khadija believed in him and encouraged him to preach his newfound faith to a few friends and neighbors.

Gradually, Muhammad publicized his teachings and tried to persuade his tribe, the Quraysh, to accept them. The new faith was called Islam, which means "submission." His followers were known as Muslims, "those who submit." The heart of this new religion was submission to Allah, the one true God. According to Muhammad, human beings have one basic choice in life. They can either accept Allah and worship him or reject him and suffer the consequences. Those who obey will be allowed into paradise on Judgment Day. Those who deny Allah will be doomed to eternal punishment in Hell. Even those who accept Islam are not automatically granted entrance to heaven. They will be judged by their good and bad deeds and rewarded or punished accordingly.

Muhammad said that throughout human history Allah had sent prophets to warn the people of God's punishment and reveal his love. A number of these messengers were sent to the Jews, including Moses, Daniel, David, and Jesus Christ, who Muhammad said was not divine but a prophet. Because Jews and Christians had not listened to or properly understood their prophets, Allah sent Muhammad—the last of his prophets—to the Arabian peoples with the true and final message. While he was a holy man, he was also a warrior, a diplomat, a husband, and a father who enjoyed the pleasures that life had to offer.

Muhammad demanded that the Arabs give up their old gods and submit to Allah. Although Muhammad first spoke to the Arabian people, Islam was a universal religion intended for everyone. Muhammad's message angered the rich and powerful people of Mecca. They were furious that he opposed the old gods. His opponents talked of killing him. In 622, Muhammad, for his own safety, migrated to the oasis of Yathrib (present-day Medina), where he came into contact with a number of Jewish tribes. He tried to convince them that he was a prophet and that they should accept him as God's messenger and convert to Islam. He said that Islam was not a new religion but a fulfillment of the Jewish-Christian tradition. But the Jewish tribes refused to give up Judaism for Islam. Muhammad then dropped some of the Jewish customs he had adopted and announced that Islam was the last prophetic revelation. It was the supreme and definitive religion. Later, Muhammad drove many of the Jewish tribes out of Medina because he felt they opposed him.

The Quran and the Sunna

Muhammad was aware that Jews and Christians had their own holy books in which God revealed himself to them. Muhammad said that Allah had revealed himself through the Quran. Since the Quran was of divine origin, not a single letter or punctuation mark could be changed.

The Quran was revealed to Muhammad in sections over a period of twenty-two years. People of the time described Muhammad as experiencing a trance whenever the Quran was revealed to him. Scribes would then copy down whatever Muhammad dictated when he came out of his trance, often writing the words on pieces of stone, palm leaves, or bone. Eventually, these were collected and organized into chapters called *suras*, and copies were made.

The word *quran* means "recitation." The Quran is a book designed not to be read but rather recited as an act of worship. The Quran is the basis for Islamic religion and morality. Out of it grew the concept of the *Sharia* (literally, the path), which is Islamic law based on the Quran, and the traditions surrounding Muhammad's words and deeds (called the *Sunna*, which means "the right way"). The Sharia was intended to regulate all Muslim behavior, including law, dress, diet, family life, marriage, relations between men and women, business practices, and religious rituals.

The Sunna also provides instruction for Muslims: Muhammad's actions and words serve as a model for the right way for Muslims to do things. The Sunna is recorded in a book of traditions called the *Hadith* (sayings of the Prophet). The Sunna is often used to clarify things written in the Quran. One example deals with *wudu*, or washing before prayer. The Quran requires a Muslim to wash before prayer, but it does not specify every detail. Early Muslims observed how the Prophet washed himself before he prayed and then imitated him. This practice is considered the Sunna of the Prophet.

The Quran, the Sharia, and the Sunna define the basic practices and beliefs of Islam despite some cultural and theological differences among Muslim communities. Selwaan Mahmoud, a Missouri college student, explains that all Muslims must practice the five basic tenets, or pillars, of Islam: a public declaration of faith (*shahada*), prayer, tithes (*zakat*), fasting (*saum*), and pilgrimage (*haj*). Says Selwaan: "Imagine a house supported by a pillar on each side and one in the center. The five tenets of Islam are like those pillars. If you take away one of them, the house will collapse."

Requirements of the Prayer Pillar

Prayer is the second pillar of Islam. To nineteen-year-old Qurat Mir, it is one of the most beautiful parts of the religion:

Almost all my prayers are filled with deep emotion. Prayer gives me a feeling of gladness and peace. I welcome the chance to communicate with him who made me and the good things he has given me. I praise God for the opportunity to live in this country as opposed to other countries. It means a great deal for me to be here. Sometimes, I find myself crying because I feel bad for those who are being oppressed.

Mazien Mokhtar did not consider himself a good practicing Muslim until he was seventeen. Now prayer is central to his life. "Prayer is our link to God. In prayer, we praise him, we remember him, we ask him for guidance and give thanks to him for what he gives us, the good as well as the bad."

Muslims are required to pray five times a day: before dawn, at midday, in midafternoon, before sunset, and in midevening. If they pray in a mosque, they will be called to prayer (a ceremony called the *adhan*) by a *muezzin*. Traditionally, the muezzin stands on top of a minaret, one of the towers surrounding the mosque. In the United States, the muezzin usually calls the congregation to prayer from inside the mosque. Five times a day, he chants:

God is great.
God is great.
I witness there is no God but God.
I witness that Muhammad is the prophet of God.
Rise to prayer.
Rise to felicity.
God is great.
God is great.
There is no God but God.

Except for Friday midday prayer, Muslims are not required to pray in a mosque. Some do, but many will pray at work, at home, on the street, in school—wherever they happen to be at the time of prayer. Inayit, whose family is Palestinian, remembers when she was a high school student and had to struggle for the right to pray during school hours:

My cousin and I were the only two Muslims in the school, and the school did not want to give us permission to leave the room to pray. Some schools set aside an empty classroom for Muslims so they can go there when it's time for prayer. Our school wouldn't at first. I told my teacher that if he wouldn't let me pray, I was going to walk out of class and do so anyway. Finally, they backed down and us go.

As noted earlier, worshipers must perform wudu, ritual washings of the face, hands, and feet, before praying. Muslims believe that worshipers should be clean when praying to Allah.

When Muslims pray, they face toward Mecca, the holy city in which the *ka'bah* is located. The ka'bah is a large building inside of which there is an ancient black stone. Muslims believe it was on this site that the prophet Abraham and his son, Ishmael, built their house in ancient times.

During prayer, Muslims recite certain passages from the Quran along with material concerning the life and deeds of the prophet Muhammad. Many Muslims have memorized the complete Quran. The prayers are accompanied by a specific number of bowings, kneelings, and prostrations. One recitation in all prayers is the *Fatiha*, the first chapter of the Quran, which reads, in part, as follows:

> Praise belongs to God, Lord of the Worlds,
> The Compassionate, the Merciful
> King of the Day of Judgment
> Tis Thee we worship and Thee we ask for help
> Guide us on the straight path
> The path of those whom Thou has favored
> Not the path of those who incur Thine anger
> Nor of those who go astray.

At the completion of the last prayer, the worshipers affirm their beliefs in the oneness of Allah and in Muhammad as his prophet and then look over first their right shoulder and then their left, saying each time they look, "Peace be on you and the mercy of Allah." This is similar to the Christian practice of shaking hands and saying, "Peace be with you."

While it is permissible for Muslims to pray in a foreign language, they are encouraged to learn Arabic in order to say the prayers in the language in which the Quran was originally revealed to Muhammad.

Most Muslims feel learning Arabic is an essential part of their religion. Ibrahim Sidicki says that all thirteen of his grandfather's children were learning Arabic by the time they were seven and that "the older generation spent a lot more time on religious matters than our generation. We have so many other things to do—work, go to school—that we can't always follow their traditions. There are many young people today who can read the Quran only in English."

A Muslim Prayer Service

Prayer may be led by an imam to keep the congregation in harmony during the service. The imam is not a priest but more of a spiritual leader. He is very knowledgeable about the Quran and Islamic law. On Fridays, the imam delivers a sermon, usually based on a passage from the Quran, just as a minister uses a passage from the Bible for his or her sermon on Sunday.

During prayer, men and women sit in separate sections in the mosque. This tradition dates to the Prophet and is referred to in the

Quran. Muslims explain that by sitting apart, the sexes are not tempted to think about each other while praying. Non-Muslims often view this practice as sexist, but this opinion is not generally shared by Muslim men or women. One man explains: "When I pray to Allah, I want to be completely focused on him. I do not want to be distracted. If a woman is seated next to me, I might think of her during prayer. It shouldn't happen, but it does. You don't always have the control over your thoughts as you would like to have."

Selwaan Mahmoud thinks that the separation of the sexes is good for both men and women: "When I am in the mosque seated among women, I feel more comfortable than if I were seated next to a man. It can be distracting, and I don't want to be distracted or cause anybody else to be distracted."

Some Muslim women in America do not feel this way, however. Anna, a computer programmer who does not dress like most Muslim women, says that she believes that the separation is discriminatory: "I pray five times a day like a Muslim should, but I never pray in the mosque and I won't until men and women pray together. If men have sexual thoughts about women in the mosque, it's their problem and they will have to answer to God for it."

Throughout the Muslim world, public services (*jumma*) are held Friday afternoon in mosques. Most men are required to attend Friday services, although women may pray at home.

The mosque is one of the unique architectural creations of Islam. The traditional mosque consists of a prayer hall and an open courtyard where people can rest and relax. The courtyard is surrounded by walls. At each corner is a minaret or tower.

Before entering the prayer hall, Muslims are required to remove their shoes as a sign of respect to Allah. There are fountains located outside the prayer room for people to wash. In the prayer hall there is a niche in the wall called a *mihrab* that marks the direction toward which the congregation faces during prayer and which is facing in the direction of Mecca. By lining up with the mihrab, Muslims are assured of facing in the right direction for prayer. Near the mihrab stands the imam, who leads the prayer and who will usually give a sermon on Friday standing in a minbar, or pulpit, which is located near the mihrab.

In the United States, most mosques are not built in the traditional Middle Eastern way. Few have courtyards. Many mosques are lofts, apartments, storefronts, and buildings that have been adapted as a place of prayer. The physical appearance of the mosque is far less significant than its spiritual meaning.

The Tithing and Fasting Pillars

After shahada and prayer comes the tradition of tithes, called zakat—the third pillar of Islam. Muslims are required to contribute approximately 2.5 percent of their salary to Islamic charitable institutions or the needy. Since many students are not wage earners, they are not yet expected to pay zakat. They do, however, perform charitable deeds (*sadiqa*). Arshia Papa is a Kansas high school senior who spends part of her time working with a youth group of Muslim teenagers in soup kitchens, retirement homes, and hospitals:

> Our youth group, which is mostly girls, visits these places and helps people. Many of them are very lonely, and they enjoy and appreciate having someone to talk to. Since many of them have never met Muslims before, we talk to them about our religion and tell them what we believe and why we dress the way we do. People often talk about what they should do to help others, but never do anything. It makes us feel good to do something.

Arshia has noticed that there is a major difference between Muslims and non-Muslims in her class regarding volunteer work: "There are others in the class who do these things to get credit so it will look good on their records for college. It's not the same feeling for us. We don't want any rewards on this earth. We do this for God's sake, because he wants us to."

Fasting, the fourth pillar of Islam, is another major obligation. Every Muslim, except children, travelers, and those who are sick, is called upon to fast from dawn to sunset during Ramadan, the holiest time of the year. Ramadan commemorates the time when Allah gave the Quran to the angel Gabriel to reveal it to Muhammad. During the fast, which lasts one month, no Muslim may eat, smoke, drink, or have sexual relations.

Fasting during Ramadan is such an important part of a Muslim's life that many individuals who stop practicing their religion still observe the practice. As one young woman explains:

> I continued to fast even though I had stopped praying and stopped going to the mosque. Fasting was such a part of me that it was almost impossible to give it up. When people saw that I wasn't eating lunch, they would ask me why and I'd say, "Oh, I'm dieting." But the truth was that it was a part of my religion that I wouldn't let go.

The Pilgrimage to Mecca

The last pillar of Islam is haj (pilgrimage). Muslims are expected to make a pilgrimage to Mecca at least once in their lifetime, if they are physically and financially able. The journey must take place after Ramadan. Haj commemorates the time when Abraham was tested by God's command that he sacrifice his only son, who Muslims believe was Ishmael. At the last minute, God sent a ram to be used as a substitute for the child.

When pilgrims approach the holy city, they all dress in white robes so that everyone is equal in the sight of Allah and there is no distinction by wealth, class, or race. In Mecca, they participate in many religious ceremonies, some of which are at the ka'bah. The cities of Medina and Mecca are considered so sacred that only Muslims are allowed to visit them.

While the haj takes place once a year, Muslims make personal visits to the holy city throughout the year and carry out many of the ceremonies associated with the haj. This visitation is called *umrah*. Umrah does not have the same religious significance as the haj and does not relieve visitors of their responsibility to eventually make a pilgrimage.

Visiting Mecca often has a profound effect on young people. Ibrahim Sidicki recalls the trip he made when he was eighteen years old:

> It was absolutely awesome. I don't know what I expected. I guess I thought I was going on a vacation. But when I saw the ka'bah, I was totally awed. To see what you've heard about all your life. And to see all the people there. I couldn't believe that people who were selling gold and silver would leave their merchandise unattended when called to prayer—and nobody would think of touching them.

Qurat Mir was in her early teens when she made umrah:

> For me it was an end point and beginning. It was a culmination of all the things I had heard about since childhood. Seeing where it all came from. Not only the places where the Prophet was but praying together with hundreds and thousands of people from all walks of life and all cultures. It made me more spiritual. It made Islam more tangible for me.

Other Beliefs in Islam

In addition to practicing the five pillars, Muslims have other beliefs that are similar to those of Christians and Jews. Like Christians and Jews, Muslims believe in Judgment Day, the time when the heavens will open and the mountains crumble to dust. Allah will then raise the dead from their graves and judge them according to their actions and deeds. Those found guilty of sinning against God will be condemned to the pits of hell (*Jahannan*), where they will be tortured throughout eternity with jets of molten bronze, fire, bitter fruit, and foul water. The blessed receive rewards in paradise (*Jannah*), where they will experience the joy of being in the presence of Allah and his angels, and fine clothes, foods, and wine.

Both men and women will be physically and spiritually perfect and enjoy each other's company. While some Muslim men give this a sexual interpretation, the Quran does not.

There are two major divisions within Islam. Over 95 percent of

Muslims are Sunnis, meaning they follow the Sunna (deeds) of the Prophet. The second major group is called Shiites, which means partisans of Ali bin Abi Taleb, the nephew of Muhammad. They believe that Ali should have been the first caliph, or commander of the faithful. Shiites also believe that there is a hidden imam, called the Mahdi, who will one day appear and bring justice to the world. Within these two groups, a number of sub-groups exist. Sometimes, there are religious conflicts between Shiites and Sunnis, but each considers the other an orthodox Muslim community. In the United States, members of both groups usually worship at the same mosque. . . .

For Anjum Mir, a student, the beauty of Islam is that it unites people of all nations, whatever their differences.

> Islam is a total way of life. We are all human beings who have been created by one God. And we are here on earth for a period. We are tried here by our good deeds and bad deeds. And we will go back again to the same God. It is as simple as that. We must get guidance, or what we do and do not do, from the Holy Quran. So when I stand before God, I can say this is the book I practiced and this is the model I followed.

THE ARRIVAL OF MUSLIM IMMIGRANTS IN AMERICA

Jane I. Smith

The presence of Muslims in America is not a recent phenome-
non, as Jane I. Smith explains in the following selection from her
book *Islam in America*. Rather, Smith reports, Muslims from various countries have immigrated to the United States for well over
a century. According to Smith, most Muslims came to America
for the same reasons as other immigrant groups: to escape religious or political persecution or to take advantage of greater
opportunities in education and employment in the hopes of
making a better life for themselves and their families. However,
she states, the experience of Muslim immigrants is also unique
because they moved to a country that was unfamiliar with and
often hostile toward their religion. Smith is a professor of Islamic
studies and the codirector of the Duncan Black Macdonald Center for the Study of Islam and Christian-Muslim Relations at
Hartford Seminary in Hartford, Connecticut.

Commentators on the emergence of Islam in the North American
scene have looked for the most part to the middle and latter part of
the nineteenth century as signaling the first real arrival of Muslims in
the United States. Indeed, at this time the first Muslim immigrants,
primarily from the Middle East, began to come to North America in
hopes of earning some kind of fortune, large or small, and then
returning to their homelands. . . .

Five Waves of Immigration

Migrations occurred in a series of distinguishable periods. The first
was between 1875 and 1912 from rural areas of what was then called
Greater Syria under the rule of the Ottoman Empire, currently Syria,
Jordan, Palestine, and Lebanon. The vast majority of immigrants from
the Middle East at that time were Christian, often somewhat knowledgeable about America because of training in missionary schools. A
small percentage was comprised of Sunni, Shi'i, 'Alawi, and Druze

Jane I. Smith, *Islam in America*. New York: Columbia University Press, 1999. Copyright © 1999 by Columbia University Press. All rights reserved. Reproduced by permission of Columbia University Press, 61 W. 62nd St., New York, NY 10023.

Muslims. By the latter half of the twentieth century that ratio was to be reversed. For the most part these early arrivals remain nameless to us, with occasional exceptions such as one Hajj Ali (rendered by Americans as "Hi Jolly"), brought by the U.S. cavalry to the deserts of Arizona and California in 1856 to help breed camels. This experiment failing, Ali is said to have stayed in California to look for gold.

The second wave came at the end of World War I, after the demise of the Ottoman Empire, which had controlled most of the Muslim Middle East. It also coincided with Western colonial rule under the mandate system in the Middle East. Many people coming to America at that time were relatives of Muslims who had already emigrated and established themselves to some degree in this country. U.S. immigration laws passed in 1921 and 1924 imposed quota systems for particular nations, which significantly curtailed the numbers of Muslims who were allowed to enter the country.

During the third period, which lasted through most of the 1930s, immigration was open specifically and only to relatives of people already living in America. The actual numbers of Muslims allowed to settle here were limited and did not rise until after World War II.

The fourth wave, which lasted from 1947 to 1960, saw considerable expansion in the sources of immigration. The Nationality Act of 1953 gave each country an annual quota of immigrants. Because it was based on population percentages in the United States at the end of the nineteenth century, however, most of the immigrants allowed to enter the country were from Europe. Still, the trickle of Muslims continued, coming now not only from the Middle East but also from many parts of the world including India and Pakistan (after the partitioning of the subcontinent in 1947), Eastern Europe (mainly from Albania and Yugoslavia), and the Soviet Union. Most of these arrivals settled in large cities such as Chicago and New York. Unlike their earlier counterparts, many of these immigrants were urban in background and well educated, and some were members of the families of former ruling elites. Often already quite Westernized in their attitudes, they came to the United States in hopes of continuing their education or receiving advanced technical training.

The last and final wave was related both to decisions internal to the United States and to events taking place in several parts of the Islamic world. In 1965 President Lyndon Johnson signed an immigration act repealing the quotas based on national diversity within the United States. For the first time since the early part of the [twentieth] century one's right to enter the country was not specifically dependent on his or her national or ethnic origin. Immigration from Europe thus declined, while that from the Middle East and Asia increased dramatically, more than half of the newcomers Muslim.

Over the last several decades, political turmoil in many countries of the Muslim world has occasioned increased emigration. In 1967 came what for Muslims was the disastrous and humiliating defeat of Arab troops at the hands of Israel, beginning an exodus of Palestinians headed for the West that has continued until the present time. The 1979 revolution in Iran and the ascent to power of Ayatollah Khomeini forced many Iranians to flee their country, a number of whom decided to come to America. Civil strife in Pakistan and the breaking away of East Pakistan to form Bangladesh, anti-Muslim pogroms in India, the military coup in Afghanistan, and the Lebanese civil war have all contributed to the Muslim presence in America. The Iraqi occupation of Kuwait led to the flight of a large number of Kurds to America, while the civil wars in Somalia and Afghanistan, the tightening of the military regime in Sudan, and ethnic cleansing in Bosnia also swelled the numbers of immigrant Muslims.

Most now come from the subcontinent of South Asia, including Pakistanis, Indians, and Bangladeshis. They first began to arrive as early as 1895 and over the century have been important in the development of Muslim political groups in America. Today this group probably numbers more than one million. Increasingly they are being joined by sizable groups coming from Indonesia and Malaysia.

Some estimates place the Iranians in this country at close to a million, with representatives of Arab countries of the Middle East, Turks, and Eastern Europeans close behind. Muslims come from a large number of African nations, including Ghana, Kenya, Senegal, Uganda, Cameroon, Guinea, Sierra Leone, Liberia, Tanzania, and many others. Naturally, these immigrants represent a great range of Islamic movements and ideologies. They are Sunnis and Shi'ites, Sufis and members of sectarian groups, religious and secular people, political Islamists and those who espouse no religious or political agenda. Many have come from circumstances in which Islam is the majority religion and find their new minority status in America difficult to adjust to. Others already know what it means to be a member of a minority religious group and come with their coping skills well honed. With each new arrival the picture of Islam in America becomes increasingly complex.

The Experience of Early Muslim Immigrants

Let us return, then, to the America of the late nineteenth century. The 1860s to the 1880s saw the first significant movement of young, relatively unskilled Muslim men, primarily from Syria and Lebanon in the Middle East. Some were fleeing conscription into the Turkish army, which they saw as little connected to their own national identities. Others had seen Christians from their homeland return from the United States with considerable wealth, and despite their reluctance to go to a setting in which they would be surrounded by non-Muslims, they were tempted to try their luck. World War I brought such devastation to Lebanon that many people were forced to flee to survive. Generally single, or at least traveling without their wives, they looked upon their time in America as only temporary, hoping that they could earn money to return and establish homes and families. Their dreams were hard to realize, however, as jobs were not easy to find in America, and often they were not able to compete for those that were available because of insufficient knowledge of English or inadequate educational preparation. Many were forced into menial work such as migrant labor, petty merchandizing, or mining. One of the most common occupations was peddling, which required little capital, language skills, or training. Working at first along the Atlantic seacoast, peddlers traveled into the South and West, often facing severe weather, thievery, and local hostility. Other Muslim immigrants served as cheap laborers on work gangs, as, for example, those contributing to the construction of railroads in the Seattle area. Women sometimes found employment in mills and factories, where they worked long hours under extremely difficult conditions. The lack of language skills, poverty, loneliness, and the absence of coreligionists all contributed to a sense of isolation and unhappiness. Compounding these difficulties was the fact that Americans of those decades certainly had little enthusiasm for foreigners, especially those whose customs seemed strange and whose religion was not Christian.

These early groups of Muslim immigrants tried to maintain a community of believers in an alien context, without institutional support. The religious training available to their children and grandchildren was minimal. They recalled that in their home countries, young people grew up with their religion in the air all around them, with holidays, festivals, prayers, and observances a constant part of the environment. America presented a different context, in which maintaining even an awareness, let alone regular observance, of the faith was obviously difficult. Neither schools nor businesses had any facilities for, nor interest in, providing opportunities for daily prayer. Those who wanted to fast during the month of Ramadan could expect no special accommodation in the workplace. Extended families to provide support and instruction were not available, and economic circumstances generally did not allow families to visit home for reinforcement of the larger familial context. Since so much of the practice of Islam is communal as well as personal, it was difficult to observe the prayers, holidays, and other Islamic occasions. The pioneer families thus had to struggle to maintain their religion and identity in a society that had been built on the backs of immigrants but that, paradoxically, had never appreciated the differences in culture that the immigrants brought with them.

Muslim Communities Across America

As the immigrants' visions of becoming rich quickly began to fade, so did their hopes of an imminent return to homes and relatives overseas. Inevitably, they were forced to adapt to a new life in their adopted

land. Young men, eager to marry and establish families, found it difficult if not impossible to locate available young Muslim women in this
country. Some went back home for brief visits to take a bride; others
had their relatives arrange marriages with girls from their home countries. In any case, traditional patterns of courtship gave way to speed
and expediency. Others married outside the faith, sometimes Arab
Christian women, although the pressures from other Muslims not to
succumb to marriage with "nonbelievers" was great.

Immigrants looked for more permanent kinds of employment,
often successfully establishing their own small businesses. Many
turned to their native cuisine as a source of revenue, founding coffee-
houses, restaurants, bakeries, and small grocery stores. Initially, these
were for their compatriots so that Muslims could at least enjoy their
own food in a culture in which so much was alien to their tastes and
traditions. Gradually, other Americans learned to appreciate Arab
cooking, and in most cities today one can enjoy Arab cooking at
everything from gourmet restaurants to fast-food joints featuring such
treats as *shawarma* (spicy meat cooked on a rotating spit and stuffed
into Syrian bread), *hummoz* (chickpea dip), and *tabouli* (chopped salad
with tomatoes, onions, and parsley).

In the first part of [the twentieth] century many Muslim families
found themselves drifting away from the faith, especially the young
people, and attempting to hide or do away with those things that
marked them as different from their American colleagues. Those
whose skin was darker than that of the average American, especially
in the South, found that they were treated as "colored" by local populations and were refused access to public facilities reserved for "Whites
only." Stereotypes of Arab Muslims as people with large black eyes,
big noses and mustaches, and ill-fitting clothes became common-
place. It became very difficult to maintain the use of Arabic as the
youth resisted speaking a tongue that sounded strange to their peers.
Their refusal to even learn the mother language was doubly painful
for their families, as Arabic was not only their cultural but their litur-
gical language. Gradually, Muslims began to choose American names
for their children or to allow the use of nicknames. Muhammad
became Mike, Ya'qub was changed to Jack, Nasreen to Nancy. Arab
and, to some extent, Muslim identity began to be something of the
past rather than the present and the future as new generations of
young people struggled to be part of the culture of their current
homeland rather than of their heritage. When these young people
matured and began to look to marriage, they turned increasingly to
non-Muslim partners, intermarriage rates rising with each generation.

At the same time, however, and to some extent in response to concerns about acculturation and secularization, in a number of places
across America Muslims began to organize into communities in
which they affirmed their identity.

THE NATION OF ISLAM

Lawrence H. Mamiya and C. Eric Lincoln

Lawrence H. Mamiya is a professor of religion and Africana studies at Vassar College in Poughkeepsie, New York. The late C. Eric
Lincoln was a professor of religion and culture at Duke University in Durham, North Carolina. In the following article, Mamiya
and Lincoln present a historical treatment of the rise of a specific
form of Islam, native to the United States and practiced primarily by African Americans. The Nation of Islam first appeared in
the early 1930s in the American heartland, the authors explain.
Its adherents, often called Black Muslims, follow a theology that
is to some degree based on traditional Islam but also differs from
it in several respects. Best known for the fiery speeches of inspi-
rational and controversial leaders such as Elijah Muhammad,
Malcolm X, and Louis Farrakhan, the Nation of Islam stresses the
importance of African American liberation, self-knowledge, and
economic independence.

In the midsummer of 1930, a friendly but mysterious peddler appeared among rural southern immigrants in a black ghetto of Detroit
called "Paradise Valley," selling raincoats, silks, and other sundries but
also giving advice to the poor residents about their health and spiritual development. He told them about their "true religion," not
Christianity but the "religion of the Black Men" of Asia and Africa.
Using both the Bible and the Qur'an in his messages, he taught at first
in the private homes of his followers, then rented a hall that was
called the Temple of Islam. This mysterious stranger often referred to
himself as Mr. Farrad Mohammed, or sometimes as Mr. Wali Farrad,
W.D. Fard, or Professor Ford.

Master Fard, as he came to be called, taught his followers about a
period of temporary domination and persecution by white "blue-eyed
devils," who had achieved their power by brutality, murder, and trick-
ery. But as a prerequisite for black liberation, he stressed the importance of attaining "knowledge of self." He told his followers that they
were not Americans and therefore owed no allegiance to the Ameri-

Lawrence H. Mamiya and C. Eric Lincoln, *Encyclopedia of African American Culture
and History*, edited by Hack Salzman, David Lionel Smith, and Cornel West. New
York: Simon & Schuster, 1996. Copyright © 1996 by Simon & Schuster and the
Trustees of Columbia University in the City of New York. All rights reserved. Reproduced by permission of The Gale Group.

can flag. He wrote two manuals for the movement—*The Secret Ritual of the Nation of Islam*, which is transmitted orally to members, and *Teaching for the Lost-Found Nation of Islam in a Mathematical Way*, which is written in symbolic language and requires special interpretation. Fard established several organizations: the University of Islam, to propagate his teachings; the Muslim Girls Training, to teach female members home economics and how to be a proper Muslim woman; and the Fruit of Islam, consisting of selected male members, to provide security for Muslim leaders and to enforce the disciplinary rules.

The Rise of Elijah Muhammad

One of the earliest officers of the movement and Fard's most trusted lieutenant was Robert Poole, alias Elijah Poole, who was given the Muslim name Elijah Muhammad. The son of a rural Baptist minister and sharecropper from Sandersville, Ga., Poole had immigrated with his family to Detroit in 1923; he and several of his brothers joined the Nation of Islam in 1931. Although he had only a third-grade education, Elijah Muhammad's shrewd native intelligence and hard work enabled him to rise through the ranks rapidly, and he was chosen by Fard as the chief minister of Islam to preside over the daily affairs of the organization.

Fard's mysterious disappearance in 1934 led to an internal struggle for the leadership of the Nation of Islam. As a result of this strife, Muhammad eventually moved his family and close followers, settling on the south side of Chicago in 1936. There they established Temple of Islam No. 2, which eventually became the national headquarters of the movement. Throughout the 1940s, Muhammad reshaped the Nation and gave it his own imprimatur. He firmly established the doctrine that Master Fard was "Allah," and that God is a black man, proclaiming that he, the "Honorable" Elijah Muhammad, knew Allah personally and was anointed his "Messenger." Prior to 1961, members of the Nation of Islam were called "Voodoo People" or "People of the Temple"; Professor C. Eric Lincoln's study *The Black Muslims in America* (1961) established the usage of the phrase "Black Muslims" in referring to the Nation of Islam.

Under Muhammad's guidance, the Nation developed a two-pronged attack on the problems of the black masses: the development of economic independence and the recovery of an acceptable identity. "Do for Self" became the rallying cry of the movement, which encouraged economic self-reliance for individuals and the black community. The economic ethic of the Black Muslims was a kind of black puritanism— hard work, frugality and the avoidance of debt, self-improvement, and a conservative lifestyle. During the forty-one-year period of his leadership, Muhammad and his followers established more than one hundred temples nationwide and innumerable grocery stores, restaurants, bakeries, and other small businesses. The Nation of Islam also became famous for the foods—bean pies and whiting—it peddled in black communities to improve the nutrition and physical health of African Americans. It strictly forbade alcohol, drugs, pork, and an unhealthy diet. Elijah Muhammad was prescient in his advice on nutrition: "You are what you eat," he often said.

In his *Message to the Black Man in America* (1965), Muhammad diagnosed the vulnerabilities of the black psyche as stemming from a confusion of identity and self-hatred caused by white racism; the cure he prescribed was radical surgery, the formation of a separate black nation. Muhammad's 120 "degrees," or lessons, and the major doctrines and beliefs of the Nation of Islam elaborated on aspects of this central message. The white man is a "devil by nature," unable to respect anyone who is not white and the historical and persistent source of harm and injury to black people. The central theological myth of the Nation tells of Yakub, a black mad scientist who rebelled against Allah by creating the white race, a weak hybrid people who were permitted temporary dominance of the world. But according to the apocalyptic beliefs of the Black Muslims, there will be a clash between the forces of good (blacks) and the forces of evil (whites) in the not-too-distant future, an Armageddon from which black people will emerge victorious and re-create their original hegemony under Allah throughout the world.

Malcolm X

All these myths and doctrines have functioned as a theodicy for the Black Muslims, as an explanation and rationalization for the pain and suffering inflicted on black people in America. For example, Malcolm Little described the powerful, jarring impact that the revelation of religious truth had on him in the Norfolk State Prison in Massachusetts after his brother Reginald told him, "The white man is the Devil." The doctrines of the Nation transformed the chaos of the world behind prison bars into a cosmos, an ordered reality. Malcolm finally had an explanation for the extreme poverty and tragedies his family suffered, and for all the years he had spent hustling and pimping on the streets of Roxbury and Harlem as "Detroit Red." The conversion and total transformation of Malcolm Little into Malcolm X in prison in 1947 is a story of the effectiveness of Elijah Muhammad's message, one that was repeated thousands of times during the period of Muhammad's leadership. Dropping one's surname and taking on an X, standard practice in the movement, was an outward symbol of inward changes: it meant ex-Christian, ex-Negro, ex-slave.

The years between Malcolm's release from prison and his assassination, 1952 to 1965, mark the period of the greatest growth and influence of the Nation of Islam. After meeting Elijah Muhammad in 1952, Malcolm began organizing Muslim temples in New York, Philadelphia, and Boston, and in the South and on the West Coast as well. He founded the Nation's newspaper, *Muhammad Speaks*, in the basement of his home and initiated the practice of requiring every male Muslim to sell an assigned quota of newspapers on the street as a recruiting and fund-raising device. He rose rapidly through the ranks to become minister of Boston Temple No. 11 and was later rewarded with the post of minister of Temple No. 7 in Harlem, the largest and most prestigious of the temples after the Chicago headquarters. The Honorable Elijah Muhammad recognized his organizational talents, enormous charismatic appeal, and forensic abilities by naming Malcolm national representative of the Nation of Islam, second in rank to the Messenger himself. Under his lieutenancy, the Nation achieved a membership estimated at 500,000. But as in other movements of this kind, the numbers involved were quite fluid and the Nation's influence, refracted through the public charisma of Malcolm X, greatly exceeded its actual numbers.

Malcolm's keen intellect, incisive wit, and ardent radicalism made him a formidable critic of American society, including the civil rights movement. As a favorite media personality, he challenged the Rev. Dr. Martin Luther King, Jr.'s central notions of "integration" and "nonviolence." Malcolm felt that what was at stake, at a deeper level than the civil right to sit in a restaurant or even to vote, was the integrity of black selfhood and its independence. His biting critique of the "so-called Negro" and his emphasis on the recovery of black self-identity and independence provided the intellectual foundations for the American black power movement and black-consciousness movement of the late 1960s and 1970s. In contrast to King's nonviolence, Malcolm urged his followers to defend themselves "by any means possible." He articulated the pent-up frustration, bitterness, and rage felt by the dispossessed black masses, the "grass roots."

As the result of a dispute on political philosophy and morality with Elijah Muhammad, Malcolm left the Nation of Islam in March 1964 in order to form his own organizations, the Muslim Mosque Inc. and the Organization for Afro-American Unity. He took the Muslim name el-Hajj Malik el-Shabazz after converting to orthodox Sunni Islam and participating in the hajj, the annual pilgrimage to Mecca. Malcolm was assassinated on February 21, 1965, while he was delivering a lecture at the Audubon Ballroom in Harlem.

From 1965 until Elijah Muhammad's death in February 1975, the Nation of Islam prospered economically, but its membership never surged again. Minister Louis X of Boston, also called Louis Abdul Farrakhan, replaced Malcolm as the national representative and the head minister of Temple No. 7 in New York. During this period, the Nation acquired an ultramodern printing press, cattle farms in Georgia and Alabama, and a bank in Chicago.

The Nation Splinters

After a bout of illness, Muhammad died in Chicago and one of his six sons, Wallace Deen Muhammad (later Imam Warith Deen Muhammad), was named supreme minister of the Nation of Islam. However, two months later Wallace shocked his followers and the world by declaring that whites were no longer viewed as devils and they could join the movement. He began to make radical changes in the doctrines and the structure of the Nation, moving it in the direction of orthodox Sunni Islam.

The changes introduced by Imam Warith Deen Muhammad led to a splintering of the movement, especially among the hard-core black-nationalist followers. In 1978, Louis Farrakhan led a schismatic group that succeeded in resurrecting the old Nation of Islam. Farrakhan's Nation, which is also based in Chicago, retains the black-nationalist and separatist beliefs and doctrines that were central to the teachings of Elijah Muhammad. Farrakhan displays much of the charisma and forensic candor of Malcolm X, and his message of black nationalism is again directed to those mired in the underclass, as well as to disillusioned intellectuals, via the Nation's *Final Call* newspaper and popular rap-music groups such as Public Enemy.

Through more than sixty years, the Nation of Islam in its various forms has become the longest-lasting and most enduring of the black militant and separatist movements that have appeared in the history of black people in the United States. Besides its crucial role in the development of the black-consciousness movement, the Nation is important for having introduced Islam as a fourth major religious tradition in American society, alongside Protestantism, Catholicism, and Judaism.

CHAPTER 2

MUSLIM LIFE IN AMERICAN SOCIETY

AMERICAN MUSLIMS FACE SIGNIFICANT BIAS

Asma Gull Hasan

The American-born daughter of Pakistani immigrants, Asma Gull Hasan is a California attorney and the author of *Why I Am a Muslim: An American Odyssey* and *American Muslims: The New Generation*, from which the following selection is taken. Hasan maintains that the greatest challenge facing Muslims in America is overcoming negative stereotypes, such as the perception that all Muslims are terrorists. According to Hasan, discrimination against Muslim Americans is widespread in U.S. society, especially because many non-Muslims have serious misconceptions about Islam and Muslims. In fact, she argues, the American Muslim community is far more diverse than most people realize. By working to correct negative stereotypes, Hasan asserts, American Muslims can strengthen their own communities and benefit society as a whole through good works and good examples.

So who are these American Muslims? And what do they want? I often heard variations on those two questions when I told people I was writing this book. When I think of my religion, I don't instantly think of the roughly six to nine million Muslims living with me in the United States—including other children of immigrants who are working for investment banks, or the numerous Pakistani cab drivers, or the prisoners who have converted to Islam. But that is my community, a large and diverse one.

The Diversity of American Muslims

For example, let's say we're looking at one block in New York City. In one building is an office for a major consulting firm, and the consultants there are busy at work. In an office in the same building, the owner of a travel agency is thinking about hiring more agents, as his business is rapidly growing. Next door is a three-star hotel, and the manager is frantically working the front desk trying to process all the check-ins and check-outs. In one of the rooms, a concert promoter is touching base with the band members he's currently working with.

On the same block, a CEO is in a 7-11 store, asking the man behind the counter if they have a particular brand of toothpaste. It is entirely possible that all the people I've described are Muslim. In fact, I personally know Muslims who fit the above profiles. Are you surprised? I guess, to some degree, I'm even a little surprised myself. But if you think about the people you know, I'm sure you've met at least one Muslim. Between you, your family, and your friends, you probably know a lot more Muslims than you realize, with more varied occupations and backgrounds than you think. American Muslims are found in all walks of life from sea to shining sea.

As for what American Muslims want, to tell the truth, they don't all want one specific political goal like electing a Muslim president or a specific social goal such as opening a mosque in every American town. We're too diverse to have one issue to rally around. For example, if all American Muslims were African-American only, they would probably focus on domestic policy and specifically issues that affect the African-American community. Though African-Americans are the largest American Muslim group, about 42 percent of the American Muslim population, they are not the entire community. South Asian Muslims are the next largest group at about 24 percent and then Arab Muslims at about 12 percent. Beyond those three major groups, people of other ethnicities also make up the American Muslim population, including white Americans, Africans, Southeast Asians, and so on. In that sense, American Muslims prove the Islamic principle of racial equality. In Islam, no race or country is favored over other races and countries. You can see from the ethnic and national diversity of American Muslims that we come from all over the globe.

The Need for Unity

Our greatest challenge is overcoming our public image as terrorists, followed closely by the need to unify, despite our different ethnicities, so that we can contribute in a significant and positive way to American society and take our place alongside other groups as a part of American culture.

That may sound scary to you: six million plus people unifying! I would be scared too, especially if I thought all these people were terrorists. I would probably write to my representative in Congress and request some action against these bad people. I would also be wary of anything they do to try to make themselves look better because I would wonder if this move was a part of their grand scheme to take over the world.

That's why I'm writing this book simply to say that American Muslims don't pose a threat to the United States or to the world. In many ways, the United States will benefit from American Muslims' attempts to strengthen their own community. For example, as Muslims unify beyond ethnicities and nationalities and create organizations in which they all work together, their experience can be a model for all Americans. In essence, Muslims' struggle to come together mirrors, or is a microcosm of, the struggle of all Americans to come together.

Negative Stereotypes

American Muslims must gain a better public image. When, for example, Mrs. Ida Smith, out in Idaho, hears of Muslims, she thinks of the World Trade Center bombing, the hostage crisis with Iran, the protests against *The Satanic Verses*, and she probably imagines that Muslims are downright un-American. Admittedly, if that was all I knew about Muslims, I would think they pose a threat to our way of life, too.

Knowing that Americans have the wrong idea frustrates American Muslims. I remember walking back to my dorm one spring day of my junior year in college and running into my good friend Lara, who had incredibly bad news. "This federal building in Oklahoma City was bombed, and they don't think there are any survivors!" she said.

"What?" I asked in shock. Like others, I first reacted to the news of death and destruction with disbelief. Lara repeated what she said and added that officials did not know, as yet, who was behind the bombing. As I internalized the seriousness of the situation, my immediate thought was, "I hope a Muslim didn't do it." Before any evidence pointing to a suspect became available, so-called experts were all over American television saying that this was the act of a Muslim terrorist and characteristic of Arab terrorism. The suited torsos and coifed hairdos of men like Steve Emerson, who were proven wrong with Timothy McVeigh's arrest and later conviction, were projected into our cozy living rooms, as they spewed tales of the characteristics of a Middle Eastern bombing fitting the Oklahoma bombing.

Between the time of the Oklahoma City bombing and the arrest of McVeigh for that bombing, there were a few moments when I had to ask myself, "Is this really happening?" I also asked myself, "I'm in the United States of America, aren't I?" What was I supposed to think when all I heard on radio and television and read in the newspapers was major anti-Islamic sentiment? During the days before McVeigh was arrested, I felt as though I was in an intellectual coma—I was the first to admit that Muslim terrorists are responsible for bad things, but I wasn't ready to condemn all of Islamic civilization merely for being Muslim.

The stereotypes that media reports spawned—that every Arab or dark, foreign-looking, bearded man or every woman in headcover is a terrorist—have consequences. How much time did federal agents lose in finding the real perpetrators while chasing bearded men? One Muslim man was detained at an airport for hours on the basis of his religion and the fact that he had ties to Oklahoma City. Muslims were treated poorly in their communities, particularly the Muslims of Oklahoma. As an American, I wanted the perpetrators caught. Additionally as an American, I didn't want to get caught up in grandiose talk of ancient hatreds, warlike ways, and tendencies for destruction that didn't find the perpetrators or lessen the suffering of the victims and their families.

At the Edge of a Cliff

With the Oklahoma City bombing, American Muslims came to the edge of a cliff and began looking over, and the bottom of that cliff is the treatment of Japanese-Americans during World War II, when they were held in internment camps, denied their rights as American citizens, and singled out as un-American. You may think I'm being dramatic, but let's analyze this situation.

My own congressman at the time, a *close* family friend who had spent much time with us, made venomous statements against the Middle East after hearing about the bombing. His statements were printed in the local newspapers.

Soon after, we received a threatening letter, directed against my family as foreigners and Muslim. This happened despite the fact that we had lived in Pueblo, Colorado, for twenty years and had many friends there.

The media frenzy against Muslims was so strong that the only question was which Islamic group was responsible—one from Iran, Iraq, or even from the United States.

What if a Muslim had done it? Islam would be confirmed as undemocratic and anti-Western. If our congressman, a family friend, could rely on stereotypes and condemn Islam (though he later apologized sincerely when my mother reproached him), how can I expect the average American to learn to distinguish between me and a terrorist, and also to realize there are a lot more Muslims like me and not like the terrorists? Even if a Muslim had been behind the blast, we, as Americans, should be smart enough and understanding enough to realize that not all Muslims would commit such acts. In fact, the vast majority never would.

American Muslims and world Muslims can't be wholly described by the "Muslim McVeighs" of their world. This has always been a problem for Islam and American Muslims: why can't non-Muslims understand that one Muslim does not represent all of us? There's always a rush to lump all Muslims together, to interpret Islam as a belligerent faith, and to characterize Muslim women as universally oppressed. Not to shock anyone, but the truth is: not all Muslims are alike, Islam advocates peace and understanding over war, and Muslim women enjoy certain rights as specified in the Qur'an. If you are a sensible person, you must ask yourself, why would a billion plus people including six million Americans subscribe to a religion that is homogenous, belligerent, and oppressive to women? That would make no sense! How could that many people subscribe to such backward philosophies? The truth is: they don't. Unfortunately, we have not asked ourselves such questions, and we continue to believe in stereotypes and misunderstandings. In fact, Islam may be the topic Americans know the least about, and misunderstand the most.

Misunderstanding of Islam and the spreading of stereotypes about Muslims are as prevalent in U.S. society as the discrimination against overweight people and smokers. Americans realize these injustices occur on a subconscious level and rarely do anything about them. I don't think Americans have intentionally declared that they do not want to know more about Islam. I do not think Americans enjoy using stereotypes and generalizations. I think they just haven't realized yet how much they don't know about Muslims.

An Uphill Battle

It's an uphill battle, but to American Muslims' credit, the hard work in improving our image has resulted in an improvement of the media's treatment of Islam. Oklahoma made the media take a deep breath and realize they had committed a grand rush to judgment. Now Muslims are not always the first to be accused by media commentators, but those commentators still have lapses in judgment and accuracy.

I know I still live in fear of anti-Muslim hysteria. Every time a bombing is suspected, on an airplane, as with TWA Flight 800, or in public places, like the Atlanta Centennial Olympic Park bombing, I, like probably all American Muslims, say to myself, "I hope a Muslim didn't do it." This thought almost precludes my sadness for the victims. It is so much easier to blame a large, ambiguous group of people who have always been seen as foreign, the "other," and so unlike us Americans, than to think of the Muslim you know personally who lives down the street or who runs the Indian restaurant you like. As a Muslim, I am very comfortable being American. I just wonder when, as a society, we'll know that Muslims are Americans too, just as there are Catholics who are Americans, Chinese people who are Americans, and so on. I don't think that's a lot to ask. I believe in Americans' ability to learn and to improve our society.

Communication: The Key to Better Understanding

The next step for American Islam is a major give-and-take between Muslim Americans and non-Muslim Americans, genuine on both sides: American Muslims must not be ashamed to educate, and non-Muslims must not be ashamed to learn. It sounds easy, but I think it's hard for one person to say to another, "Can I ask you some questions about your religion?" It's also easy to become frustrated if one is trying to explain something and one's listener continues to resort to stereotypes.

I remember once in college my roommate, Alexandra, dragged me to a showing of final projects from the video production class. One was a series of interviews of various people, edited together. I knew one woman because she was in my gay literature class, and I presumed she was a lesbian, though I didn't really bother to ask because I didn't think it was my business.

I was a little intimidated by this woman and others in the class because they seemed to project a coolness I couldn't comprehend. I was quite convinced I was the only straight woman in the class. At that, I wasn't even a highly experienced straight woman! So there I was, probably the only straight woman in a class of lesbians and bisexual women, and I myself had the least amount of practical knowledge about sex! This class would make even the most unassuming person self-conscious.

So, in this film, about midway through it, the woman in my class said: "I really don't know what it's like to be a Muslim woman, to be a woman in that culture." This shocked me! I had no idea she was curious about being a Muslim woman. I then felt a little embarrassed because, even if she had dozed through most of our gay literature classes, she should have an idea I was Muslim since I was constantly using American Muslims in examples and arguments. Why hadn't she asked me this question?

The film ended, and I saw that the woman was sitting in the row in front of me. I walked down my row and sat down in a seat behind her and tapped her on the shoulder. She turned to see who was tapping her, and, with her scarf and dark glasses, she evoked for a moment the glamour of fifties' movie stars.

"Hi!" I said, "I just wanted to tell you that I am a Muslim woman, and I would be happy to talk to you at any time about being Muslim and female."

"Oh," she said nervously. Then she just giggled, almost out of embarrassment. She didn't say anything, so I added something like, "Well, give me a call, if you want," and left.

I never heard from that woman, ever. I was surprised, too. At Wellesley, we were constantly encouraged to share with one another, and I was certainly ready to share and learn. Yet, this woman wasn't. I have no idea why she didn't call me, and why we didn't chat about things. It wouldn't have been easy for me either, but I thought it would be useful for both of us to talk about something she had questions about, and I had some answers for. I was hurt, too. I thought I had made an effort to listen to others in our class, but this woman couldn't do that for me.

I eventually told my mother how disappointed I was that this woman and I hadn't ever spoken. I told my mom that I felt as though she had played on people's stereotypes of Muslim women for shock value, to make herself look inquisitive, sensitive, and intelligent. But when push came to shove, she really *didn't* want to know what it was like to be a Muslim woman. Her comment was just superficial.

"No!" my mother replied excitedly. (For a second I thought my mom was going to say that this woman must have had a crush on me and was too embarassed to talk to me.) "Asma, if this woman said that, it means she must have thought about it a little bit first." My mom persuaded me that somewhere in this woman's brain curiosity on the subject of Islam had registered, and that was a good start. "If a lesbian, somebody outside of mainstream society, is curious about Muslims," my mom said, "then everybody else must be too." I liked my mom's more optimistic and mature view of this woman: I want to believe that Americans and others are interested in Muslims beyond mere shock value.

AMERICAN MUSLIMS DO NOT FACE SIGNIFICANT BIAS

Daniel Pipes

Daniel Pipes is the director of the Middle East Forum, a Philadelphia-based think tank that works to define and promote American interests in the Middle East. He is a columnist for the New York Post *and formerly served in the U.S. Departments of State and Defense. His books include* The Long Shadow: Culture and Politics in the Middle East *and* The Hidden Hand: Middle East Fears of Conspiracy. *In the following excerpt from* Militant Islam Reaches America, *Pipes argues that reports of widespread bias against Muslims in America have been blown out of proportion. In reality, he asserts, American Muslims are flourishing socially, financially, and politically. Pipes cites examples and statistics to bolster his claim that Muslim Americans have not been victimized but actually have been fairly accommodated by workplaces, schools, the media, and the courts.*

President Bill Clinton in early 2000 stated that American Muslims face "discrimination" and "intolerance." Not long after, the U.S. Senate passed a resolution inveighing against "discrimination and harassment" against American Muslims.

These pronouncements did not happen by themselves, but followed on years of effort by organizations claiming to speak on behalf of Muslims living in the United States. Thus, the American Muslim Council (AMC) complained of an "ongoing wave of discriminatory acts." The Council on American-Islamic Relations (CAIR) went further, stating that "discrimination is now part of daily life for American Muslims." And a member of the CAIR board, Mujeeb Cheema, found that Islamophobia, or the hatred of Islam, is "at epidemic levels in the West." But these are mere statements, not proofs of bias. Do American Muslims really face more obstacles than other Americans as they go to school, make a living, and express their faith?

In fact, a review of American Muslim life—based largely on information made available by CAIR and other Muslim organizations— finds a flourishing community that rightly boasts substantial accomplishments. The picture is far better than the self-appointed Muslim groups would have us believe.

Positive Experiences

In socioeconomic terms, Muslims have little to complain about. They boast among the highest rates of education of any group in the United States, with a 1999 survey finding that 52 percent have a graduate degree. Among converts, whites tend to be highly educated, blacks not. That said, Muslims among African-Americans are substantially better educated than their non-Muslim counterparts.

Education translates into prestigious and remunerative work. Immigrant Muslims concentrate in the professional and entrepreneurial vocations, with a specialty in engineering and medicine. A 1970s survey found 17 percent of Muslims in the United States to be engineers and 13 percent in medicine. A 1980s inquiry found a quarter of Muslims working as engineers and 8 percent in medicine. A 1990s survey in Chicago found 17 percent engineers, 8 percent in medicine. A late 1990s national survey found 20 percent engineers and technicians, 14 percent medical. Though the numbers range considerably, they consistently point to a disproportionate number of Muslims in these professions.

More than a few American Muslims have lived out the classic immigrant success story of arriving with a few dollars and building up substantial wealth. Average income for Muslims appears to be higher than the U.S. national average: a 1996 survey found them with a median income of $40,000 (versus $32,000 for the country as a whole); among African-Americans, Muslims have a median income of $30,000 (compared with $23,000 for all blacks); this same research found 70 percent of Muslim with incomes over $70,000. A 1999 survey of 878 Muslims found 38 percent reporting a household income of over $75,000. A year later, the median yearly household income was said to be $69,000. One specialist, Abdulkader Thomas, notes that "As a rule, upper-income Muslim immigrants tend to be conspicuous consumers," and indeed, Muslim magazines are replete with advertisements for luxurious mansions, stately cars, and fine jewelry.

Business tycoons of note include Bijan (high-end men's clothing), Rashid A. Chaudhry (personal care products), Ayhan Hakimoğlu (military contracts), Yusef Haroon (consulting and managerial services), Mansoor Ijaz (investment management), Farooq Kathwari (furniture), Nemir Kirdar (venture capitalism), and Safi Qureshey (computers). The very richest American Muslim appears to be a software engineer of Turkish origins, Kenan Sahin, who netted $1.45 billion in 1999 on selling his company, Kenan Systems (which specializes in billing plans), to Lucent Technologies. American Muslims proudly say that theirs is "the richest Muslim society on earth," and they are right.

These, in short, are not an oppressed people.

Fighting Bias, Finding Goodwill

Further, the Muslim effort to be accepted in the United States is not a particularly difficult one, for enlightened Americans make persistent efforts to understand Islam and portray Muslims positively. This results from a sense of guilt about past prejudice, plus a multiculturalist impulse. Jewish and Christian groups often join with Muslim counterparts to fight what they perceive as bias. For example, when Representative James Rogan (Republican of California) refused to meet with a Muslim leader, Salam Al-Marayati, on the (correct) grounds that Al-Marayati "seems to be an apologist for Muslim terrorists," Jewish and Christian organizations rushed to Al-Marayati's defense and held a news conference that was instrumental in prompting Rogan to back down and apologize to Al-Marayati.

Similarly, Muslims in the dock often find themselves benefiting from the pro bono services of non-Muslim lawyers, sometimes eminent ones intent on winning justice for them. And where money is needed, non-Muslim institutions come to their aid; the Becket Fund [which describes itself as] "a bipartisan and ecumenical, public-interest law firm that protects the free expression of all religious traditions," helped a Muslim police officer in Newark, New Jersey, win a case in Federal Appeals Court that entitles him to wear a beard.

Less formally, too, one finds innumerable expressions of goodwill. Some citizens delight in the appearance of mosques, for example, as articulated by one resident of Frederick County, Maryland, during a debate about a zoning request for a mosque: he hoped the structure would be built because "a mosque will be an asset for not just the Muslim community, but the entire community." Non-Muslims occasionally even donate funds to construct mosques, something that invariably astonishes immigrant Muslims, who have no prior experience with such ecumenism.

The U.S. government has taken steps to recognize Islam. In 1990, President George Bush began the custom of congratulating American Muslims on the occasion of the Islamic holidays. A year later, Muslim men of religion began the practice of opening sessions of Congress with recitations from the Qur'an. The president, the first lady, and the secretary of state have all hosted Muslim delegations to celebrate the breaking of the Ramadan fast. In 1996, Vice President Al Gore became the highest-ranking American official to visit an American mosque. In 1997, the National Park Service installed a star and crescent in the Ellipse Park near the White House, along with the National Christmas Tree and a Hanukkah menorah. When the first Muslim ambassador was appointed in 1999 to represent the United States to Fiji, he took the oath of office by swearing on a Qur'an.

The U.S. military has been forthcoming to Muslims. In 1992 a military aircraft took seventy-five enlisted Muslim soldiers to Mecca for the pilgrimage. In 1993 a first Muslim chaplain was commissioned by the U.S. Army, and a second one in 1996—the first ever American chaplains to be not Christian or Jewish. The armed forces provide halal meals for Muslims and do not require daily physical training during Ramadan. . . .

Public Expression of Islam

When observant Muslims seek to live by the precepts of their religion, especially in the workplace and in schools, the picture again is a positive one, judging by what one sees in connection with Islamic holidays and prayers, as well as men wearing beards and women head coverings.

The Islamic holidays present two challenges: based on a lunar calendar, they move forward each solar year by about ten days, making it impossible to schedule an annual time for them; and while there are only a few main holidays, one of them (Ramadan) lasts a month, during which pious Muslims fast during the day and carouse at night—customs not exactly conducive to work. Several corporations—including Northrop—permit their Muslim staff to work a shortened day during Ramadan. Getting employers to permit several days off during two of the other holidays, called the Eids, has not always proven easy, but one American employer after another has acquiesced in this demand, including the Larus Corporation. Several school districts, such as New York City's, permit Muslim students to be absent on five Islamic holidays; Paterson, New Jersey, is unique in actually closing its schools for the two Eids. Some corporations—notably Northrop—allow Muslim employees to take off the several weeks or even months required to make the full-scale pilgrimage to Mecca.

Muslims are required to pray at five designated but changing times through the day. Although it is permissible to make up the prayers at a later time, many pious Muslims insist on praying exactly on time. If they work or attend school, this means fulfilling two conditions: getting time off and finding a suitable venue. Remembering that there are millions of American Muslims, the problems are relatively few in number; they tend to involve factories, where it is difficult to let employees take off at times of their choosing.

Muslim plaintiffs at times win substantial settlements against employers for prayer-related issues. In Lincolnshire, Illinois, Mohammad Abdullah's habit of leaving his job at about noon on Fridays for prayers caused him to be fired, even though he arrived early to work or stayed late to compensate. After taking his case to the Equal Employment Opportunity Commission (EEOC), he won a $49,000 settlement in 1997. In Jacksonville, Florida, Fareed Ansari won $105,216 from Ray's Plumbing Contractors, his former employer, for firing him when he insisted on leaving work early on Fridays to attend the weekly prayer service. . . .

Issues of Appearance

Wearing a beard has great symbolic importance for some Muslim men, being a way to emulate the Prophet Muhammad and signal membership in a pious community. This was the case, for example, for Pakistani-born Mohammad Sajid: "It was a big thing for me. I was afraid of a new society. It was just like [being in] a jungle." But because, against corporate rules, he insisted on wearing a beard, he was briefly dismissed as a dishwasher at a fast-food eatery in Sacramento. Eventually, however, Sajid got his job back, as did Muslim males at such companies as Adirondack Transit Lines, Coca-Cola, Hilton Hotels, McDonald's, Safeway Inc, and Taco Bell.

When a Muslim goes to court over this issue, he invariably wins. The Minnesota Unemployment Appeals Court decided in favor of a fired Muslim who refused to shave his beard, ruling him entitled to receive unemployment benefits from his employer, Sims Security/ Burns International Services. The EEOC found that United Parcel Service discriminated against a beard-wearing Muslim in Illinois by refusing to promote him to a driver's position. A Federal Appeals Court backed a Muslim policeman in Newark, New Jersey, entitling him to wear a beard and receive $25,000 in back wages, finding that the police department's policy "violates the First Amendment."

The usual modesty issue concerns women wearing the *hijab*, a cowl-like headscarf that covers the hair. For Muslim women, this fabric serves as a sign of reserve and a means of self-identification. For American employers, it is occasionally perceived as mildly offensive or an impediment to customer relations. When they demand its removal, the Muslim women frequently protest or file discrimination law suits, again with considerable success. In March 1999, after apparently being fired from their jobs with Argenbright Security at Dulles International Airport screening passengers and baggage, five immigrant Muslim women filed a suit with the EEOC, claiming that having to remove their scarves violated the 1964 Civil Rights Act. The two sides settled out of court, with the women receiving written apologies, $750 in back pay, $2,500 in additional compensation, their jobs back, and the company promising to provide religious sensitivity training at all of its U.S. locations. . . .

Modesty issues also arise in schools, where students dressing modestly occasionally—but only briefly—run afoul of dress codes. A Muslim girl attending high school in Fort Worth, Texas, won permission to wear a *hijab* while playing soccer. High school students in Williamsport, Pennsylvania, won the right to have their mandatory swimming instruction in private. A Muslim boy at the Lincoln Middle School in Gainesville, Florida, was sent home because he would not tuck in his shirt, as the school dress code demanded; when the student's parents argued that long, loose-fitting, and untucked shirts are more modest, the school permitted this exception. A female applicant to The University of Health Sciences in Kansas City, Missouri, requested not to be palpated (physically examined) by male colleagues; the school initially declined her application, but then reversed its decision and accepted her, although this meant disrupting the usual practice of having medical students learn from examining each other. . . .

Disrespect for Islam

Muslims are undoubtedly right when they say that Islam suffers from a poor reputation in the United States. But they cannot complain about receptivity to their complaints. Public figures who make statements perceived as inimical to Islam by Muslim groups usually apologize right away. Two days after Senator Joseph Biden, Jr. (Democrat of Delaware), worried on television that bombing Iraq might "embolden Islam to become more aggressive with the United States," he contradicted his words: "Islam is one of the world's great religions. It stands for peace, tolerance, and justice and it is responsible for many enlightening advances in human thought and practice over the centuries."

When the media offends Muslims or makes a factual mistake, an apology or retraction follows with (uncharacteristic) speed. Jay Leno of NBC's *Tonight Show* apologized for a seemingly inoffensive comedy sketch about an imaginary amusement park in Iran and promised to be "more diligent in the future." Martin Goldsmith, host of National Public Radio's *Performance Today*, related a legend about the Prophet Muhammad relying on special coffee to "make love to forty women in one night" over forty nights. He soon offered "sincere apologies" for giving offense and thanked his listeners for making their concerns known. After Paul Harvey, said to be the most listened to radio broadcaster in America, called Islam a "fraudulent religion," he quickly dubbed this an "unintentional slur" and duly apologized on air for having "understandably offended" Muslims. . . .

The Internet follows these same special rules for Muslims, who are protected from the sort of things routinely said about blacks or Jews. AT&T WorldNet Service removed a site that defamed the Prophet Muhammad as a "rapist" and found him worse than Adolf Hitler. GeoCities took down a Web site that called Islam "a threat to the whole world" and profaned the Prophet ("Mohammed The Playboy" and "Prophet Mohammed's Libido Exposed!"). America Online closed down a site that published pseudo-Qur'anic verses, on the grounds that it was "clearly designed to be hurtful and defamatory." This is not prejudice but kid-glove treatment. . . .

Employees with grievances sometimes make out well in court. Lule Said, a Somali immigrant, was working in 1991 as a guard for Northeast Security of Brookline, Massachusetts, when a co-worker complained about his origins and faith, announced that he hated Muslims, wiped his feet on Said's prayer rug and kicked it aside, then threatened him. Said complained to his supervisor but was told to stop praying or he would lose his job. The Massachusetts Commission Against Discrimination awarded Said $300,000 (about a decade worth's of his salary) for these tribulations and chewed out Northeast Security: "This case uniquely demonstrates . . . the debilitating impact discrimination has on an individual's well-being." Ahmad Abu-Aziz, an immigrant from Jordan, claimed that from the start of his employment for United Air Lines in California in 1994, he faced discrimination—being compared to a terrorist, his name ridiculed, derogatory comments about his religion and national origin, unfair work assignments. When Abu-Aziz complained to his supervisor, he was ignored, then terminated for supposed misconduct. He went to court and a jury awarded him $2.9 million in damages, a sum sustained by appellate court.

In other words, just as American Muslims have benefited from multiculturalism, so they are benefiting from the government readiness to dictate workplace rules.

Recognizing Fortunate Circumstances

American Muslims fully recognize their fortunate circumstances. A mid-1980s survey found that "No Muslim interviewed reported that he or she had ever experienced any personal harassment in the workplace or knew of any experienced by a friend or associate as a result of being either Muslim or foreign-born. Nor did any of those interviewed report any problems in buying or renting homes or apartments as a result of perceived prejudice." An early 1990s study into Muslim youth found that all the women interviewed "denied they were oppressed in any way in the United States." In 2000, an AMC poll found 66.1 percent of Muslims agreeing with the assertion that "U.S. society currently shows a respect towards the Muslim faith."

Individual Muslims concur. Fereydun Hoveyda, a former Iranian official now living in New York, finds that in the United States "there is no animosity at all to Islam." Jeffrey Lang, the Christian-born professor of mathematics, writes of his conversion to Islam: "I do not believe it has greatly affected my career." "Our life in this county has been terrific and we love it," an immigrant to Virginia named Hisham Elbasha tells *The Washington Post*. Muslims also note that bias is diminishing; in 1999 a young Muslim in Washington said he witnessed "increased tolerance observing the month of Ramadan this year."

Even those same Muslim organizations that complain about discrimination and "Islamophobia" sometimes admit that things are going well. Ibrahim Hooper of CAIR, one of the most vocal supporters of this position, acknowledges that "Domestic policy towards the Muslim community is quite good." His boss, Nihad Awad, makes a similar point, that "here anti-Muslim feelings have no roots, unlike Europe." Institutionally, CAIR finds that things are better in the United States than in some Muslim countries: "Muslims in America," it has said, "take for granted rights routinely denied to their co-religionists in Turkey." Khaled Saffuri of the Islamic Institute goes further, conceding that in the United States, "there is relatively speaking a better degree of freedom compared to many Muslim countries." It all sounds very good indeed.

Limited Bias

All this is not to deny that some bias against Muslims does exist. But no immigrant group or non-Protestant religion is wholly free of this. Buddhists and Hindus, adherents of religions yet more alien to most Americans, also face prejudices and are subjected to ridicule. Their temples are on occasion vandalized with swastikas smeared on temple walls, with one attack specifically timed to take place on the anniversary of *Kristallnacht*, the Nazi rampage against Jews in 1938. Buddhists and Hindus do not receive the favorable media treatment accorded Islam. Yet they hardly complain, much less do they have a protest industry.

Further, what bias against Muslims does exist is contained, illegal, and of relatively little import. Linda S. Walbridge, an anthropologist who immersed herself in an American Muslim community, offers a useful comparison with anti-Catholic sentiment: the latter "has not disappeared from America, but it is at a low enough level that it certainly does not hinder Catholics from participating in all spheres of activity. There is no reason to think that Muslims . . . will experience anything much different." Adjustment is needed, to be sure, to accommodate a new and still alien faith: employers have to learn about beards, head scarves, prayers, and fasts; advertisers will take a while to understand Muslim sensitivities. Nonetheless, the record shows an impressive flexibility on the part of American institutions, public and private, to acknowledge Islam and oblige Muslims. To help the process along, Muslims have considerable sway over the media and are in the process of building an impressive lobbying organization.

If one were to speculate about the reasons for this happy circumstance, two explanations spring to mind. One is American openness to the immigrant and the exotic, combined with a historic disposition to offer a level playing field to all. The other is a genuine multiculturalism—not the specious doctrine of racial and ethnic "diversity" imposed so successfully on American institutions but a sincere willingness to accept and learn from other civilizations. Other factors play a part as well, including the growth of the regulatory arm of government and especially its readiness to dictate workplace rules. American Muslims have been quick to avail themselves of these benefits, as is, of course, their right.

It is also the right of CAIR, AMC, and the Muslim Public Affairs Council to devote their resources to promoting the idea of Muslim victimization. They do so for the same reasons that some other ethnic and religious defense groups do—to pay the bills and fuel the grievances they hope to ride. But the reality is stubbornly otherwise: far from being victimized, the Muslim American community is robust and advancing steadily. For non-Muslim Americans, the lesson should be clear: even as they continue to welcome active Muslim participation in American life, there is no reason to fall for, let alone to endorse, spurious charges of "discrimination and harassment."

THE NEW ISLAM

Carla Power

Some of the strongest challenges to stereotypes of Muslims are coming from second-generation Muslim Americans, as *Newsweek* reporter Carla Power explains in the following article. These young Muslims, she relates, are equally at ease with their centuries-old faith and the contemporary popular culture of America, their country of birth. They have an increasing impact not just on American perceptions of Islam but on their faith itself: Power writes that many in this subculture of young American Muslims have reexamined and reinterpreted basic texts to discover a religion that allows for, and is in accord with, modern notions of equality. Although the younger generation has encountered some of the same types of discrimination as did their predecessors, the author concludes, they nevertheless have a strong sense of confidence that has begun to manifest itself in the exercise of greater political clout.

In El Cerrito, Calif., Shahed Amanullah knows it's time to pray, not by a muezzin's call from a mosque minaret, but because his PowerMac has chimed. A verse from the Koran hangs by his futon. Near the bookcases—lined with copies of Wired magazine and Jack Kerouac novels—lies a red Arabian prayer rug. There's a plastic compass sewn into the carpet, its needle pointing toward Mecca. At the programmed call, Amanullah begins his prayers, the same as those recited across the globe—from the Gaza Strip to Samarkand.

In his goatee and beret, 30-year-old Amanullah wouldn't remind anyone of Saddam Hussein or a member of Hizbullah, the sort of Muslims who make headlines. He has never built a biological weapon, issued a *fatwa* or burned Uncle Sam in effigy. "You think Muslim, you think Saddam Hussein, you think ayatollah," says one Muslim-American twentysomething.

Not after meeting Amanullah. A native Californian, Amanullah grew up running track, listening to Nirvana and reading the Koran. He is a member of a burgeoning subculture: young Islamic America. The children of the prosperous Muslim immigrants of the '60s and

'70s are coming of age, and with them arrives a new culture that is a blend of Muslim and American institutions.

Online and on campus, in suburban mosques and summer camps, young American Muslims are challenging their neighbors' perceptions of Islam as a foreign faith and of Muslims as fiery fundamentalists or bomb-lobbing terrorists. That image problem may be this generation's biggest challenge in the New World. Within hours of the Oklahoma City bombing in 1995, Muslims were prime suspects. "You'll die," was one of the printable messages left on mosque answering machines around the country.

America's Muslims are not only taking on stereotypes, they're taking on the status quo. As it was for Christians and Jews before them, America is a laboratory for a re-examination of their faith. America's Muslim community is a quilt of cultures: about 25 percent are of South Asian descent, Arabs represent another 12 percent and nearly half are converts, primarily African-Americans. U.S. society allows them to strip away the cultural influences and superstitions that have crept into Islam during the past 1,400 years. By going back to the basic texts, they're rediscovering an Islam founded on tolerance, social justice and human rights. Some 6 million strong, America's Muslim population is set to outstrip its Jewish one by 2010, making it the nation's second-largest faith after Christianity. Richer than most Muslim communities, literate and natives of the world's sole superpower, America's Muslims are intent on exporting their modern Islam. From the Mideast to central Asia, they'd like to influence debate on everything from free trade to gender politics.

At home, it is a generation committed to maintaining its Islamic heritage while finding a niche in the New World. America's 1,500-odd mosques are spread from Alaska to Florida. Muslims pray daily in State Department hallways, in white-shoe corporate law firms and in empty boardrooms at Silicon Valley companies like Oracle and Adaptec. Last year Muslim organizations made life miserable for Nike when the company marketed a shoe with a design resembling the name of Allah in Arabic. After protests, Nike discontinued the style and started sensitivity training for employees. In Washington, the American Muslim Council lobbies on issues from school prayer to the Mideast peace process. "We're learning to use our clout," says Farhan Memon, a Muslim and 27-year-old partner in Yack!, a multimillion-dollar Internet publishing business.

Clout doesn't come without confidence, says Manal Omar, a Muslim woman raised in South Carolina. Tall and leather-jacketed, with a trace of Southern drawl, she explodes any stock image of the crushed and silent Muslim woman. In high school, she played basketball in *hijab*— the Muslim woman's head covering ("my coach nearly freaked"); at college, she won national public-speaking prizes. Friends thought she should become a stand-up comic. Instead, Omar went into refugee relief. In her off hours, she's working on a series of books for Muslim-American teenagers—"a sort of Islamic 'Sweet Valley High,'" she says.

If fighting stereotypes is American Muslims' biggest battle, it is women who are on the front line. Raised playing touch football and reading *Seventeen* magazine, women are returning to the Koran to discover whether Islam sanctions the veils, seclusion and silence that many Muslim women endure. (Short answer: no.) In Afghanistan or Saudi Arabia, wearing a veil is the law. In Savannah, Ga., or Topeka, Kans., it's a statement. "For some young women, the veil in America works a bit like the Afro during the black-power era," says Mohja Kahf, a professor at the University of Arkansas. Amira Al-Sarraf, 34, a teacher at an Islamic school in Los Angeles, explains: "I don't have men flirting with me. I enjoy the respect I get."

At her wedding four years ago, Amanny Khattab wore an Islamic veil under her translucent lace tulle one. She remembers the "living hell" of her freshman year at Farmingdale High School on New York's Long Island. "The week before school started, I bought all the cool stuff—Reebok sneakers, Guess! jeans," recalls Khattab. "I wanted to look just like everybody else, but with the scarf." It didn't work. But enduring all the cracks—"towel-head," "rag-head"—made her tough. "Non-Muslim women think I'm oppressed because I wear too much?" says Khattab. "Well, I think they're oppressed because they wear too little."

In Pakistan, tradition dictates that women pray at home rather than at the mosque. In America, women not only go to the mosque—they're on the mosque's board of directors. Saudi Arabian clerics have ruled that it's un-Islamic for women to drive. But try telling a 16-year-old from Toledo, Ohio, who's just gotten her driver's license that the Koran prohibits her from hitting the road. She'll probably retort that the Prophet's favorite wife, Aisha, once directed troops in battle from the back of a camel.

That willingness to challenge convention is revitalizing a religion that many think has stagnated since the Middle Ages. Today a reformation is afoot. Muslims worldwide are working to square a faith founded in Arabia with modernity. Debates rage: Is Islam compatible with Western-style democracy? With modern science? With feminism? American Muslims, wealthy, wired and standing on the fault line between cultures, are well positioned to bring a 13-century-old faith into the next millennium.

The United States is arguably the best place on earth to be Muslim. Multicultural democracy, with its guarantees of religious freedom and speech, makes life easier for Muslims than in many Islamic states in the Middle East. It's an idea they'd like to export. U.S. Muslim social organizations send money and medicine to beleaguered Kashmiris and Bosnians. The Web site of the Minaret of Freedom Institute, an organization devoted to "promoting the establishment of free trade and justice," has links to the Islamic University of Gaza. "The U.S.

Constitution describes the perfect Islamic state," says Muhammed Muqtader Khan, who teaches American politics to Muslims. "It protects life, liberty and property."

Growing Muslim-American political consciousness may be the surest sign of assimilation. While their parents may have been happy to sit on the sidelines and pine for the Old World, the new generation realizes that to protect its rights as Americans—and Muslims—it has to speak out. Some mosques educate their communities to be more politically assertive, registering voters and holding programs on how to be an active PTA parent. Freshly minted Muslim lawyers are joining other ambitious young politicos in Washington. "When people say we'll never have elected Muslim-American officials, I say, 'Hey, those are the same things they said about a Catholic named Kennedy running for president'," says Suhail Khan, a 28-year-old congressional staffer. Muslim and Arab groups have protested against airport-security profiling, which they say unfairly targets them as potential terrorists. Last month the American Muslim Council organized a fax-and-phone campaign against bombing Iraq. The No. 1 foreign-policy concern is the Arab-Israeli peace process. Recently, the Arab American Institute—which involves both Muslims and Christians—took a congressional delegation to Syria for a 3½-hour meeting with President Hafez Assad to discuss the issue.

In the 1996 election, three times as many Muslims supported Bill Clinton as Bob Dole. The White House has not forgotten. Last month the First Lady threw a Ramadan party in the marble-and-gilt Indian Treaty Room in the West Wing. Hillary Clinton's talk—which touched on everything from peace to democracy to the trials of being a beleaguered minority—drew fervent applause. Long after the First Lady left, guests loitered, munched baklava and hummus and took snapshots of one another. Having made it to the White House, it seemed, they didn't want to leave.

Muslim Students: The High School Experience

Richard Wormser

Reporter and author Richard Wormser interviewed dozens of young Muslim Americans for his book American Islam: Growing Up Muslim in America. *In the following selection, Wormser focuses on the experiences of high school students (some of whom requested that only their first names be used). Wormser reports that many Muslims attending public high schools are subjected to slights against their religion by both teachers and fellow students. At the same time, however, some Muslim students establish meaningful friendships with non-Muslims, fostering a better understanding of Islam. Wormser describes students' experiences with discrimination, their attempts to challenge stereotypes, and their relationships with non-Muslim students.*

The rumor had spread around the school since Tuesday. A Muslim girl, no one knew who, had been walking home from school when a car suddenly pulled alongside her. A male student she didn't know jumped out and ripped the scarf off her head, blew his nose in it, threw it back at her, jumped back in the car, and drove off, leaving the poor girl in tears.

The problem was that nobody knew if the story was true. Anam, whose family had come to America from Pakistan, felt that even if it wasn't true, it could have been. The World Trade Center in New York had recently been bombed. [The first World Trade Center bombing, in which six people were killed, occurred on February 26, 1993.] People had been killed in the explosion and "Muslim fundamentalists" had been arrested and charged. The air was tense and Anam could sense that when people looked at her, their looks were not friendly. And so she made a major decision:

> As a Muslim woman, I am required to cover my hair. We do this to avoid attracting men and engaging in flirtations. It is a way of protecting us. In my parents' country, all women are covered, so none of us stand out. But in America, being covered makes you stand out. I am a very religious person, but I

do not want to draw attention to myself. So I decided not to wear my hejab in public.

Anam's problem is one that is shared by many young Muslim women. While their religion requires them to be covered, they feel they need to make compromises for reasons of personal safety.

Although Muslim students are not usually bothered in school, harassment can suddenly escalate in times of crisis. Several Muslim students in southern high schools were slammed against lockers and walls during the Gulf War. Sadeck, a ninth-grade student in New Jersey, remembers how painful it was for her to go to public shool after the World Trade Center bombing. "The kids would call me towel-head," she says, "and threaten to remove my hejab to see if I was bald."

In Washington, D.C., two young Muslim women were bumped by a man who deliberately crossed the street to walk into them. In Michigan, a female student tried to pull a hejab off the head of a Muslim student and discovered, to her astonishment, that Muslim women are not necessarily pacifists. "She didn't mess with me anymore after that," the Muslim student recalls, adding, "We are taught to avoid fighting if we can, but if we can't, then we should avoid losing."

Most Muslim students learn to handle the petty annoyances from other students without too much difficulty if the behavior is childish and not vicious. Muhammad Jihad, a student in Ohio, says that after a bomb exploded on a Pan Am jet over Scotland [in 1988], killing everyone on board, a fellow student asked him if he was the guy who planted the bomb. "It was a stupid thing to say, and I felt as bad as anybody. In fact, I think I felt a lot worse than most." Another student says that when she first entered high school and wore a hejab, some students spread a rumor that she was receiving chemotherapy for cancer and that she covered her head because she had lost all her hair. "It was dumb, but that's the kind of thing you have to put up with if you're a Muslim." Tehani El-Ghussein recalls that she was friendly with a Jewish student who sat behind her in class: "I hadn't covered when I first was in class, so he didn't know I was Muslim. Then, when I decided to cover, he was shocked. He asked me if I was Muslim, and I said yes. 'Aren't we supposed to hate each other?' he said. He was kind of kidding, and we were friendly afterwards, but it was never the same."

When the Teacher Is the Problem

Some students have problems with their teachers. A few teachers are openly hostile to Muslims. One student remembers how a teacher once remarked, "Your people are enemies of the United States." Other teachers, while not expressing their hostility openly, do so in subtle ways. Deena, who eventually left public school to attend a Muslim school, was denied permission to take advanced courses even though her grades made her eligible. "My teacher never said why he denied me," she says, "but I was sure that it was because of my religion."

Malal Omar, an honor student and an excellent basketball player, remembers how she and her friend Inayet had to overcome their coach's prejudices:

> We were both good enough to be starters. But we did not wear the usual basketball shorts and short sleeves that the other players wore because we are Muslims. Instead we kept our head covered and wore loose clothing when we played. Our coach, who was male, didn't understand this. When we went out on the court he said, "Come to the sidelines, what are you doing there?" At first he didn't play us. He kept us on [the] bench for a while, which was a downer, a blow to our egos . . . but when he saw that our dress didn't interfere with our playing, he was cool.

Some teachers perpetuate the stereotypes that all Muslims are rich oil sheiks and terrorists. Other teachers who discuss Islam or the Middle East in class often get the facts wrong. One student recalls sitting in class listening to the teacher giving incorrect information about Arab history: "I wasn't strong enough to speak out. So I sat there listening to all those distortions, burning inside." Another Muslim student, Mai Abdala, took the opposite position at her school: "When a teacher made a mistake, I spoke up—and said too much." Another student reports: "I had a teacher who called my religion Mohammedanism. I corrected him, and he got angry. He showed me a book in which the term was used. I said, 'Yes, but this book was written by a Western man a long time ago who didn't understand us. We don't worship Muhammad. He was a prophet, not a God. It offends us when somebody calls us Mohammadans.' The teacher accepted the criticism, but he wasn't happy about it. I had to work real hard to keep my A in his class."

Far more difficult to deal with are the teachers who sometimes try to embarrass a Muslim student or express hostility to Muslims. Most Muslim students try to explain their position in class, but by doing so they run the risk of becoming the target of the teacher's anger—and receiving poor grades. Selwaan Mahmoud had one teacher who she felt was hostile: "I would talk in class about Islam. Nothing political, just trying to explain the religion. Then my history teacher would say, 'Well what about Iran and Iraq?' Or he'd make a remark that women have to walk ten feet behind men. He was either ignorant or just trying to annoy me."

Challenging Assumptions

Many people believe that Muslim women are restricted if not oppressed by men. This is true in some countries where the patriarchal tradition is strong, modernization is limited, and religious fervor is high. Historically, Islam improved the condition of women at the time of the prophet Muhammad by guaranteeing them certain basic rights, and ending female infanticide, which some of the desert clans practiced. Today, middle-class women in most Muslim countries enjoy a wide variety of rights. (This isn't always the case for poorer women.) All of the young Muslim women interviewed for this book strongly denied they were oppressed in any way in the United States. Anjum Mir remarked: "People are very appearance-oriented. They don't understand it. They have to be educated. We don't feel subjugated. Separation makes us feel more equal. We feel men respect us as a person, not as a sexual object."

Qurat Mir gets annoyed when people judge her and her friends on the basis of her appearance and stereotypical notions:

Just because we are covered and don't date and sit separately from men in the mosque or in class, people say we are oppressed. That's just not so. Just because a woman wears sexy clothing, does that make her free spirited? Just because we wear loose clothes and are covered, does that make us oppressed and sedated? The only true freedom for me is freedom of the mind. Not being trapped by your body frees the mind. By being covered the mind shows. People deal with you for what you are, not how you look.

Rania Lawendy, a college student who is invited to high schools to speak to students about this issue, shares Qurat's feelings:

I don't feel Western women are free. Muslim women had the right to have property and vote long before Western women could. When a woman's money was her husband's in the West, Muslim women kept whatever they earned. I don't think it's freedom to show off your body. American women need to be educated. No one can tell me that they're more free than I am!

Earning Respect from Non-Muslim Friends

. . . Even though their beliefs and behavior are different from those of non-Muslims, and despite the occasional problems that arise, Muslim students, for the most part, enjoy public school and make good friends there. Ayesha Kezmi recalls that her non-Muslim friends helped her assert her identity as a Muslim: "I did not cover my head until I was in high school. Although I felt myself a sincere Muslim, I did wonder about the kind of life other students were living. Interestingly, it was my non-Muslim friends who encouraged me to assert my identity as a Muslim. I strongly believe that you can't stay to yourself. You have to have both non-Muslim and Muslim friends."

Some students believe that their friends show them more respect

because they're Muslim. Joshua Burt notices how his friends' behavior
has changed: "If they cuss, they apologize right away. I like that
because it shows respect for me. They're sorry almost before it comes
out of their mouth. So it helps them. They don't cuss so much. I also
notice that they also drink less. If we're out together, they may drink a
Coke instead of a beer because they know my religion forbids alcohol."
Rania was elected senior class president in her high school even
though there were no other Muslim students in attendance. "I feel
they elected me," says Rania, "because they know that as a Muslim, I
don't lie, I don't cheat, and I can be trusted to keep my word." She
finds that her girlfriends trust her with their secrets and talk to her
about their fears: "Because I'm a Muslim, they know I won't try and
steal their boyfriends and I could look at things objectively and tell
them the truth." Kalil says that his classmates even help him to be a
better Muslim: "I notice that during Ramadan, they try and help me
keep my fast. They don't eat around me, and some of them even try to
fast with me for a day or two. They try to keep me in check." Tehani El-
Ghussein remembers that when she was about to enter high school,
she felt a great deal of anxiety about covering her head. Her best friend,
who was not Muslim, said, "Hey, do it! That's your religion. It's cool."

Muslim Students Face Difficulties

Some Muslim students find that practicing Islam in a non-Muslim
country is hard. Anjum Mir notes that "America is the best place to
practice Islam. You have a freedom here that you won't find in many
places. But to be a Muslim in America, you need support. It's very difficult if you're alone. You need to practice with others."

Muslim students often think that they must act as a model for others. As one teenage girl put it: "If you do not carry yourself as a good
Muslim, you give Islam a bad name. When people see how I act, they
see I have a moral code. I once found $100, and I returned it. Some of
the kids thought I was crazy. Then I heard someone say, 'Oh, she's a
Muslim.' What that means to me is that I fear God."

Sometimes, Muslim students feel a certain degree of alienation
from non-Muslim students, who are much less serious than they are.
Qurat Mir found many of her fellow high school students to be "hol-
low. I really saw people around me only concerned with petty things,
how they looked, about their dates, things like that. It bore no rele-
vance to the kind of life I wanted for myself.". . .

Most Muslim students are comfortable with their religion and with
being Muslim in a society that is often in conflict with their values.
Suzani says, "I love Islam. Islam is a way of life, not just a religion. It's
my language, my culture, my history, my morals. I consider myself a
Muslim-American, and when people ask me which side of the hyphen
is stronger, I say, 'I love America and I owe a lot to this country, but I
am a Muslim first.'"

MUSLIMS ON CAMPUS: BALANCING RELIGION AND COLLEGE LIFE

Beth McMurtrie

For many American students, college is a time of exploration and independence. The question for Muslim students, as Beth Mc-Murtrie relates in the following article, is how best to reconcile the liberal culture of the college campus with the observance of Islamic beliefs. Typically, she notes, Muslim college students from traditional backgrounds are required to dress modestly and are forbidden to drink, date, or even associate with members of the opposite sex. These students often find it difficult to explain their religious obligations to non-Muslim students, the author reports. In addition, McMurtrie writes, Muslim students follow different levels of adherence to Islamic regulations. Students who are less traditional—for example, women who choose not to wear a head covering—may find themselves isolated from their fellow Muslims as well as the non-Muslim majority. McMurtrie is a reporter for the *Chronicle of Higher Education*.

Amina Fahmy grew up in Egypt, in a devout Muslim family, accustomed to a society in which single men and women do not hug, let alone date. When she arrived at George Washington University, she discovered she had been placed in a coed dormitory reputed to be one of the most promiscuous in the country.

Samiya Mohiuddin's mother did not want her to wear a *hijab*, or head scarf, fearing her daughter would be subject to the kind of discrimination she had faced as a young Indian doctor. Devout, but afraid of becoming an outcast, the younger Ms. Mohiuddin sat in her car for three hours at the beginning of her freshman year, a *hijab* wrapped around her head, before she gathered the courage to step out.

Yasir Qureshi liked to party. Raised in a nonobservant family in New York, he became curious about Islam after a friend quit drinking and began praying. But he was turned off by the more observant Mus-

Beth McMurtrie, "For Many Muslim Students, College Is a Balancing Act," *The Chronicle of Higher Education*, vol. 48, November 9, 2001, pp. A55–A57. Copyright © 2001 by *The Chronicle of Higher Education*. This article may not be published, reposted, or electronically redistributed without express permission from The Chronicle. Reproduced by permission.

lims at George Washington, whom he felt were narrow-minded and judgmental. He drank, but wasn't he Muslim, too?

Islam on Campus

Islam is often portrayed as monolithic, insular, and extremely conservative—a view reinforced since the September 11 attacks. But the truth is as complex as the lives of the people it enfolds.

Less than 1 percent of American college students today are Muslim. About half of those are from predominantly Muslim countries like Pakistan and Egypt—some the children of wealthy businessmen, others political refugees. The rest are American, often the children of immigrants.

Although Muslims are the most visible religious minority on college campuses, their conflicts—with society, their faith, and each other—are rarely noticed by outsiders.

For many, Islam requires modest dress, a ban on alcohol, prayer five times a day, and limits on dealings with the opposite sex. Even handshakes and eye contact can be off-limits. Such constraints turn daily life into an obstacle course. Meanwhile, those who do not abide by religious laws often feel pressure from Muslim peers to conform to orthodox teachings.

States with large Muslim populations, such as California and Texas, tend to attract the most Muslim students. The District of Columbia is no exception: George Washington University draws about 900 Muslim students from the United States and abroad. They are comfortable in this metropolitan area, which is home to 150,000 Muslims and more than a dozen major mosques. "You can't walk the streets and not see women wearing head scarves," says Anisah Bagasra, a senior from New Jersey.

Each Friday afternoon, a Presbyterian church on the campus's edge opens its basement for Jumma, a weekly communal prayer service that draws about 300 people. The student union houses a Muslim prayer room, allowing students to stop by between classes for any one of five prayers required daily. Nearby markets cater to students who eat food prepared according to Islamic law. And during Ramadan, a holy month in which people fast between sunrise and sunset, the Muslim Students Association holds a group dinner several times a week.

Adapting to College Life

Yet even on a campus with so many accommodations to Muslim life, challenges abound. When Ms. Fahmy discovered where she had been assigned to live, she almost refused to move in. But her father reassured her that she could handle it.

Now happily ensconced in Thurston Hall, Ms. Fahmy says her adjustment was easier than she expected. She credits her multidenominational roommates—one Greek Orthodox, one Jewish, and one not religious—who aren't bothered by her dawn prayers, or her refusal to date or drink. But they don't hesitate to tease her about her sheltered upbringing.

"We like to shock her all the time," jokes a roommate, Lauren Bacalis. "We watch *Sex and the City.*"

"Oh God! I still can't believe that!" Ms. Fahmy says, jumping up from the couch in her dormitory room. A collection of videotapes of the graphic HBO series, which depicts the sex lives of four single women, sits on the bookshelf behind her.

She admits to watching the show. But when it gets too racy, she says, "I make little excuses to go into the closet."

Ms. Fahmy has adapted in other ways. She downloaded a program onto her laptop computer that issues the call to prayer several times a day. She is used to seeing men visit her roommates, although she's not quite comfortable with the idea.

If anything, her faith has deepened. In a predominantly Muslim country like Egypt, she says, religious devotion is taken for granted. Here, she must be deliberate.

"A lot of people here are really put off by religion or God, whether it be Islam or Christianity or Judaism, and that really surprised me," she says.

Their notion is that "religion and being an intellectual, or someone who actually thinks rationally, don't go together. I was like, no, I don't want to become [like] that."

The tight-knit Muslim communities found on many campuses are both a refuge and a source of stress. Students say it's a relief to be around others who intuitively understand the nuances of being Muslim—at George Washington, men get together to play basketball every week and women gather to study or talk. At the same time, there's more pressure to conform.

Several students at George Washington say fellow Muslims lectured them after they were seen in bars or spending time with people of the opposite sex. Mr. Qureshi, who graduated in the summer of 2001, was one of the few less-observant students contacted who agreed to be identified in print. "I consider myself Muslim," he says, "but not practicing every day."

Shania Flagg, a senior at George Washington, is not surprised by that reticence. "A lot of people don't want to reveal their lifestyles because they don't want to be criticized or ostracized," says the New Jersey resident, who stopped drinking and dating when she converted to Islam as a teenager, but has male friends and goes to bars to shoot pool. "It's kind of like the 1950s. Everybody pretends it's all good and happy and everybody's religious."

To non-Muslims, the Islamic community can appear closed off. Angela Caras, a convert to Islam and a law student at the University of Texas at Austin, explains that it's hard to be devout without observing some social limits. Having lived among Muslims for several years now, the Texas native is struck by how much her non-Muslim classmates talk about sex. "I feel almost like an outsider," she says.

"Men Are from Marwa"

Relationships between men and women can be particularly complicated. At a conference for Muslim students held at the Massachusetts Institute of Technology [MIT in October 2001], the liveliest session was "Men Are from Marwa, Women Are from Safa," a play on a popular book about relationships, in this case referring to two sacred hills in Mecca. Seated on opposite sides of the room, men and women poured out their confusion. Is shaking hands OK? Can a woman ask a man to help her with her homework? Is casual conversation sinful?

One young woman complained that Muslim men often avoided Muslim women yet joked with non-Muslim women. "It's like: You're wearing a *hijab*, get away from me," she griped. A young man said that it was the women who were skittish. "The moment the aura of marriage is in the air, Muslim women run away with leaps and bounds," he said, to laughter.

Asma Syed, a junior at the State University of New York at Buffalo who attended the session, says that especially for women, it is hard to find the line between being friendly and compromising one's beliefs.

Ms. Syed, who moved from Kashmir to New York when she was 13, has to explain to men why she cannot shake hands, and tries to gently deter non-Muslims who attempt to tell crude jokes in front of her. In movie theaters, she turns her head during romantic scenes, and she has had to tell more than one flirtatious male classmate that she simply does not date. "We have to do a lot of reasoning every day," she says.

Yet she is hardly shy. The former president of the Muslim-students association at Buffalo, she once ran after a male classmate to chastise him for not saying hello. He explained that he was afraid she would consider him too forward if he greeted her.

Thinking About Marriage

For many, college is a time for social and sexual exploration. But some Muslim students face a different kind of pressure, as their parents urge them to marry. Because dating is discouraged, many students are eager to comply in order to find companionship, says Ms. Bagasra, who is in charge of outreach for the Muslim Students Association at George Washington.

Traditionally, parents play an active part in finding a mate, although Ms. Bagasra says it's not unusual for college students to meet someone they're interested in, then notify their parents. Once that happens, the couple is allowed to become acquainted in the company of chaperons.

Arranged marriages, however, are not uncommon. Ms. Mohiuddin, the George Washington student who agonized over wearing a head scarf, got married during the summer after her freshman year. Her husband proposed through a relative, after viewing Ms. Mohiuddin, a Maryland resident, while she was on a family trip to India. They had never talked, although he was a friend of her cousin's. After her parents made some inquiries, she went back to India and spent two days with him before she agreed to the marriage.

"My roommate was, like, you just talked to him and said yes? But it's more than that," says Ms. Mohiuddin, shy and giggly, as she sits in the small apartment she shares with her sister. "I know my parents wouldn't have chosen him if he was not good for me."

In Islam, she explains, love does not precede marriage but grows out of it. "The whole thing about religion, I think, is that once I'm married, I'm automatically going to love him because we're going for the same goal."

Islam has gained a reputation as being hostile to women, an idea Muslim college students constantly try to refute. Sanam Nowrouz-zadeh, a senior at George Washington, has become adept at fielding questions on whether her head scarf is a sign of oppression. She says it is simply an "outward symbol of faith" and notes that Islam grants women the rights of inheritance and divorce, and the right to pick her mate—pretty revolutionary ideas when they first appeared, in the seventh century.

Although some double standards remain—men are more likely to date than women are—others are dissolving. Women frequently hold leadership roles in Muslim campus organizations, for example. A generation ago, those groups were dominated by men.

While some Muslims try to maintain conservative traditions within the liberal culture of college campuses, others want to make room for individuality within the orthodoxy.

Zafar Shah, a senior at the University of Texas at Austin, was raised in a devout household in Texas, but has largely rejected the conventional practice of Islam. He dates, he does not fast, and he rarely associates with other Muslims. But, he argues, he is no less Muslim than his classmates who pray five times a day. He says his activism on behalf of the poor, immigrants, and gay people—even though homosexuality is a sin, according to the Koran—is a reflection of those aspects of Islam that espouse tolerance and equality for all.

"Being Muslim to me, in the United States, it's about believing in opposition and in struggle, and it also incorporates a sense of being part of a community," he says. "The things I do, in terms of social-justice activism, I don't look at that as being separate from being Muslim."

Yet Mr. Shah says he feels rejected by more traditional Muslims. One painful episode occurred in a course he took . . . on the practice of Islam in the United States. "Everyone was Muslim. Everyone was very pro-Islam," he recalls. "I was the only naysayer in the entire class."

During one session, the class discussed *The Satanic Verses*, a novel by Salman Rushdie that many Muslims find offensive. Of 65 students, Mr. Shah says, he was the only one to defend Mr. Rushdie's work. The professor flippantly asked if he had ever been to a mosque. Mr. Shah realized that his professor and classmates probably assumed he was not even Muslim. "It really hurt me in a way that I didn't think was possible," he says. "I feel marginalized in the mainstream society, and I have to feel marginalized in the Muslim community."

Speaking Out

Despite their small numbers, Muslim students' clout on campuses is growing. Dozens of colleges have built prayer rooms. Dartmouth and Mount Holyoke Colleges have dining halls that serve halal food. Syracuse University suspends classes for Eid Ul-Fitr, the end of Ramadan.

That influence extends to political activism. Many students have spoken out on behalf of Muslims in Chechnya, Iraq, and the West Bank, to counter what they view as hostile actions by the U.S. government. At the University of California at Davis, for example, a student group for Palestinian rights erected nearly 500 cardboard tombstones on the campus in the spring of 2001 in memory of Palestinians who had died in recent clashes with Israel.

Some international students say they are disappointed by how little their American classmates seem to know about the Muslim world. Rida Barakat, a senior at George Washington and a Palestinian who grew up in Jerusalem, says Americans are quick to associate his countrymen with suicide bombings, yet don't bother to learn much about the conditions that would inspire such extreme action.

Other students, particularly those raised in America, focus on giving Muslims a voice in domestic politics.

Fatima Khan, a senior at Boston University who interned in the summer of 2001 in Sen. Edward M. Kennedy's office, hopes to work for a nonprofit organization dedicated to human rights or environmental issues. She says people need to understand that being Muslim and American are not mutually exclusive. "I feel as a public servant, as someone trying to help the environment, that is Islamic," she says. "But that is also American."

A session on political activism at the MIT conference reflected the ambivalence among many Muslim college students toward the U.S. government. Several people were openly skeptical of evidence blaming Middle Eastern Muslims for the September 11 attacks. Others wondered whether they could get involved in politics without becoming complicit in U.S. foreign policy, which they saw as anti-Muslim

Islands of Tolerance

Since September 11, many Muslims say they have noticed a tremendous surge of interest about Islam.

Samrana Ihsan, a senior at the University of California at Davis, says the Muslim Students Association there usually has to beg people to attend Islam-awareness events. These days, the group is "overwhelmed" with requests for information.

Although a number of students have reported incidents of harassment in recent weeks, by and large, they say, college campuses tend to be islands of tolerance.

For the many Muslims who have relatives in both the United States and abroad, this is a particularly confusing time. In mid-October [2001] Ms. Bagasra, the George Washington senior, received an e-mail message from her husband, who lives in Pakistan. He asked her permission to fight a jihad, or religious battle, against any nation that sent ground troops into Afghanistan.

His request was not unexpected. Ms. Bagasra had visited Pakistan a few weeks earlier, and knew that Islamic clerics there were telling people that they must defend their Muslim brothers and sisters against foreign invaders.

She wrote back, explaining that a jihad does not require one to take up arms, and that he could do his religious duty by helping Afghan refugees. She feels conflicted, she says, because she is both American—her mother is German-Irish—and Muslim.

As she tells her story, Ms. Bagasra sits at a table in the small Starbucks inside George Washington's student union. She thinks a minute about the incongruities in her life. Her classmates are agonizing over midterms, while she faces the continuing possibility that her husband will go to war.

How did a religion that had been so personal to her become so political? Her friends keep asking her what it all means.

"You know, I really can't say right now," she later admits. "Because I'm still struggling to figure things out for myself."

MUSLIMS IN THE AMERICAN WORKPLACE

Marc Adams

Many Muslim Americans feel uncomfortable in their workplaces, and religious discrimination and bias complaints from Muslims at work are on the rise, Marc Adams observes in the following article. According to Adams, the source of the majority of these problems may be employers' unfamiliarity with Islamic practices and customs. He asserts that greater understanding of the religious obligations of Muslim employees is necessary in a diverse workplace. For example, he explains, Muslims are required to pray several times a day, a practice that most companies could easily accommodate by allowing short prayer breaks. Working to increase understanding and making reasonable accommodations for religious practices, the author concludes, can benefit both employers and employees. Adams is a freelance business and legal affairs journalist based in Winchester, Virginia.

Lobna "Luby" Ismail awoke before dawn in her hotel room near Orlando, Fla., knelt on the floor and bowed low in the direction of Mecca to say her morning prayers. She finished dressing, wrapped her Muslim head scarf, or *hijab*, snugly around her dark features and, after a light meal, headed off to lead a cultural training session at Walt Disney World Resort.

Ismail sat in silence in the front of the room while the trainees, all of them Disney World employees, arrived. She then scrawled a message on the blackboard: "The first part of this session will be nonverbal, OK?"

As the students nodded in agreement, she wrote another message asking the trainees to share with their training partners, in writing, some assumptions that society—or the class members themselves—might make about a woman who looked and dressed like she did. Responses ranged from "submissive" and "uneducated" to "foreign" and "someone who is not my friend."

Ismail then broke the silence by proclaiming in perfect English that

Marc Adams, "Showing Good Faith Toward Muslims," *HR Magazine*, vol. 45, November 2000, pp. 53–55, 60. Copyright © 2000 by the Society for Human Resource Management. Reproduced by permission.

she is a born-and-bred American who was the pitcher for her ninth-grade softball team and student body president in high school and who today is a wife and business owner.

"People don't realize that many Muslims in this country are American," says Ismail, a partner in Connecting Cultures, a Silver Spring, Md.–based consulting firm that specializes in diversity training.

Ismail is one of many advocates engaged in a burgeoning campaign to pierce the stereotypes about Islam and its followers, called Muslims. These advocates want to help employers make their workplaces more comfortable for the country's growing numbers of Muslims, who may be of any race or from any part of the world.

A Growing Force

The U.S. government does not collect census data on religion, so there is no official count of how many Muslims are in the United States or how their numbers have grown. According to the American Muslim Council, a lobbying group based in Washington, D.C., there are about 6 million Muslims in the country today. The council has no data on the number of Muslims in the workplace but it estimates that the overall Muslim population has jumped by 1 million since 1995. That growth rate—coupled with a rising tide of religious accommodation complaints from Muslims—suggest that the Muslim workforce is growing and is increasingly vocal, experts say.

According to a 1999 survey conducted by the Tanenbaum Center for Interreligious Understanding, based in New York, 76.5 percent of Muslim respondents were at least somewhat troubled by religious bias at work—the highest rate of concern for any of the religious groups surveyed, including Buddhists, Hindus or Jews. And 27 percent of Muslims said they had run into discrimination personally or knew other Muslims who had—second only to Hindus at 32 percent.

The study, which focused on employees who are members of minority religions, also shows that 63.7 percent of Muslim respondents felt very comfortable at their workplaces. But that means more than one-third of respondents were not comfortable—a rate that Muslim advocacy groups say is too high.

Experts say that, if anything, the Tanenbaum study shows that employers still are coming to grips with religious accommodation and that acceptance of Muslims' strict religious code is an important test of employers' commitment to diversity.

"All it takes is being aware of these issues and a willingness to deal with them," says Ibrahim Hooper, communications director of the Washington, D.C.–based Council on American-Islamic Relations (CAIR), a leading Muslim support group that mediates workplace complaints. "We haven't yet come across a situation that can't be resolved to the satisfaction of both parties."

The challenge for human resource professionals is how to accommodate Islamic religious practices that, to many employers, seem out of place at work.

For example, Muslims' hallmark head scarves, skull caps, turbans and beards may clash with uniforms or the crisp, office attire that portrays a company's image. Muslims also pray several times a day and must attend Friday midday services, which can disrupt schedules and work flow. Some Muslims might avoid sustained eye contact or decline to shake hands with members of the opposite sex, practices that might be viewed by other employees as impolite or even biased in today's workplace culture, where body language can be a vital part of business communication.

"We had the case of a [Muslim] doctor who was called for a job interview across the country," Hooper recalls. "The employer had arranged for his air fare, the rental car—the whole thing." When the doctor informed his prospective employer that he refrains from shaking hands with women, the employer called him back and told him the interview was off, Hooper says.

Experts point out that Muslim behavior and dress aren't attempts to flout workplace policies but are based on strict Islamic tenets of modesty and respect. Muslim advocacy groups, such as CAIR, say that one of their biggest tasks is explaining those tenets to employers and correcting false impressions of Islam.

But the groups say they also spend a lot of time reminding businesses that, under Title VII of the 1964 Civil Rights Act, religious accommodation isn't optional. The law requires employers to accommodate sincerely held religious beliefs unless the accommodation poses "undue hardship," which generally is measured by the arrangement's cost. For example, suppose you have to hire a temporary worker to replace an employee who is absent for religious reasons. If you're paying top dollar for the temp and you have to do it often, you can probably claim undue hardship.

And what constitutes a "sincerely held belief"? The answer can depend on who is talking. For example, some Muslims say that certain practices, such as wearing beards or avoiding touching or making eye contact with members of the opposite sex, are customs, not religious requirements. Other Muslims look on these practices as mandated by their religion. Legally, it doesn't matter. If it's the employee's sincerely held religious belief, the employer has to accommodate it, according to guidelines from the U.S. Equal Employment Opportunity Commission (EEOC).

Muslims' Complaints Rise

Increasingly, Muslims' struggle for acceptance in the workplace is framed in terms of employee complaints. At the EEOC, Muslims' share of total religious discrimination complaints rose from 12 percent in 1992 to 15.5 percent in 1999. Those figures don't count other complaints that never get as far as the EEOC but that instead are mediated by Muslim groups. At many companies, accommodations have resulted from agreements with CAIR after rugged play in the media.

Most of the complaints CAIR receives are lodged against supervisors who don't allow prayer breaks or who say that company dress codes prohibit women from wearing head scarves. The problem, Hooper says, usually is not corporate policies but individual supervisors' lack of knowledge about religions and religious accommodation law. Typically, once a dispute arises, companies' executives accommodate the employees and end up apologizing for supervisors who were not aware of the firms' accommodation policies, CAIR officials say.

"Employers have to stop making these innocent mistakes—they have to know more," says Ismail. "Asking a Muslim woman to remove her head scarf is like asking a woman to take off her blouse."

Understanding also works both ways. Some employers claim that Muslim workers take prayer breaks or change from business dress to Muslim attire without notice. Muslim advocacy groups agree that there is work to be done on both sides.

For example, while CAIR publishes a detailed guide for employers on how to accommodate Muslim practices and garb in the workplace, neither CAIR nor the American Muslim Council sponsors forums or seminars to help employers anticipate the more complex accommodation issues before they boil over. "We could do more in that area," says CAIR spokesman Ismail Royer. On the other hand, with a caseload of about 50 complaints a month, CAIR is forced to spend most of its time dousing brush fires.

"None of these problems is insurmountable in terms of undue hardship," Hooper says of Muslim accommodation issues. "I mean, you have Sikhs wearing turbans, Amish women wearing bonnets, Orthodox Jewish women wearing scarves or covers over their hair. I think people just have to realize that American society is becoming more diverse. Any employer who doesn't deal with that is going to be left behind."

CHAPTER 3

MUSLIM AMERICAN
WOMEN

Contemporary Issues
Companion

American Muslim Women: Between Two Worlds

Asma Gull Hasan

One of the more persistent stereotypes of Islam is that it fosters the oppression of women. In the following selection from *American Muslims: The New Generation*, Asma Gull Hasan, a Muslim woman who grew up in Colorado, challenges this stereotype. While she concedes that women in some Islamic countries are relegated to a subservient role, Hasan argues that such treatment is more cultural than religious. She maintains that passages in the Koran have often been misinterpreted to support the oppression of women. However, she notes, Muslim American feminist scholars are working to promote more accurate translations of these passages and to rediscover Islam's tradition of supporting woman's rights. Hasan is a California attorney and the author of *Why I Am a Muslim: An American Odyssey.*

I was debating with my extended family once during a family gathering whether Muslim women and men should be allowed to pray in the same room. I reasoned that on Judgment Day men and women will stand equally before God with no gender preference. My grandfather piped up, "No, men are superior in Islam!" We were in my uncle's normally quite noisy Suburban, which had now gone silent at my grandfather's words.

My family members waited a moment, and then said things like, "Oh no!" and "You're in for it now, grandfather!" They were saying all this because I am known in my family for responding vehemently to such statements. I stayed levelheaded, however, and asked my grandfather, "You mean in the Qur'an?"

"Yes!" he said.

"I don't think so," I said.

"No, it says it!" he retorted.

After a few minutes of this yes-no business we finally got to the merits of the argument. My grandfather felt that since God's messengers were all male, men must then be superior in God's eyes. I countered that a woman, Khadijah, Muhammad's wife, was the first convert

Asma Gull Hasan, *American Muslims: The New Generation.* New York: Continuum International Publishing Group, Inc., 2000. Copyright © 2000 by Asma Gull Hasan. All rights reserved. Reproduced by permission.

71

to Islam. Without her faith in Muhammad, *no Muslims would exist.*

I offered other arguments proving gender equality in Islam, but something told me that my points were falling on deaf ears. I joked that my grandfather must have received the Taliban version of the Qur'an. The Taliban are the Islamic revolutionaries who took over the Afghanistan government and banned women from working because they said that was against their interpretations of the Qur'an. The country came to a near stand-still as half the professional population—doctors, teachers—were not allowed to work. Obviously, the Taliban had to modify some of their policies to keep the country functioning. The Taliban validly has pronounced that they put an end to Afghanistani tribal practices which hurt women. They were forced to marry and had no right to property or divorce. So as unenlightened as the Taliban is, they have actually elevated Afghanistan's rural population.

Though I tried to make light of the situation, I was saddened that *my own grandfather* would say such a thing, even if he believed it. Does he really think that I, as a woman, am inferior to my brother, merely because he's male? I see in my grandfather the effects of South Asian culture, which is patriarchal, on his interpretation of the Qur'an. Sure, there are a few passages that taken out of context, interpreted from a patriarchal perspective, or not updated for our times (which the Qur'an instructs us to do) imply women's inferiority. They are by no means passages on which to build tenets of Islam, however. When I asked my grandfather to show me where in the Qur'an it says that women are inferior to men, he replied that it would take him some time to find the passage. As he has still not found it, I presume it doesn't exist or isn't clear in its meaning.

But this is what it came to—my own grandfather, a product of his society and prejudices, saying that women are inferior to men. This despite the fact that women outnumber men in his own family. He has five granddaughters and three grandsons—it's in his interest to see women as equal to men! It hurts, but I understand that we all have to read the Qur'an and make our own interpretation. This is my *jihad* with my grandfather. Who knows—maybe someday my grandkids will disagree with me on a belief, emphasized by my American culture, on something similar.

Culture and Status

The debate over the status of women in Islam is probably the best example of how culture affects interpretation. Men like my grandfather have taken a few Qur'anic passages and, coupled with a patriarchal culture, have interpreted them in the most literal and self-serving way. It happens in all cultures, not just among Muslims, and such chauvinism existed before Islam, perhaps even before organized religion itself. There is no Islamic basis for demeaning women or oppressing them. Culture is the culprit here, and no one really is immune from that.

American culture often favors men and holds women back. Women are paid less than men for similar jobs. We have yet to elect a female president. We're still arguing over a woman's right to control her body. Sexual harassment and rape are very difficult to prosecute. Office politics, sometimes on a subliminal level, keep women from rising to top positions. However, no one sees the American woman as being as severely oppressed as the Muslim woman. Women *are* oppressed in *some* countries where the majority of the population is Muslim. There, women's literacy rates are often quite low, among many other disadvantages for advancement.

However, such oppression is not mandated by the Qur'an. It is in fact condemned by it. Furthermore, strong Muslim women are all over the place. Benazir Bhutto became the prime minister of Pakistan twice, which is more than we can say for a female politician in the United States. Muhammad's wife Khadijah, was one of the most successful business people in Mecca. Fatima Mernissi is one of the most intelligent Islamic scholars and a prominent thinker, and she is a woman. My own mother runs the lives of our family as well as being a dynamic volunteer worker and fundraiser. My dad calls her "the boss" and sometimes a tyrant. Here I am writing a book on Islam in America. Do I seem oppressed to you?

The challenge women like my mom and I face is to overcome the cultural baggage that haunts American Muslim women. Though women in Islamic countries are often oppressed, Islam as a philosophy is very pro-woman. However, as with all philosophies, societies, and cultures, contradictions occur in the journey from paper (Qur'an) to practice (my grandfather). Because of these contradictions, Muslim women all over the world are being pulled in two different directions: one is to fulfill the traditional expectations for a Muslim woman, like marriage at a young age and raising a family; the other to explore the new roles for women in the modern world by being career women and community activists.

The problems we face—in trying to express our feminism, become activists, and be independent—are acute versions of what American women in general are going through. As more American women convert to Islam and more young Muslim women like me grow up, it is in our interest, as Americans, not to be like my grandfather and rely on what we have heard through the grapevine, but to encourage all women to explore their identities and their strengths, and instill in them the belief that they can contribute to our society, our economy, our values as much as men can.

A Diverse Group

Who is the American-Muslim woman? The Islamic Council of New England Conference (ICNE) on "Women in Islam" said all Muslim women should be knowledgeable about Islam and become mothers.

Women are also expected to be modest and keep interaction with males to a minimum, making activities outside the home difficult. According to Aminah McCloud, these aspects associated with the term "Muslim woman" arrived upon the American scene with Muslim immigrants in the later part of the twentieth century; these immigrant Muslim women wore strict Islamic dress and were committed to raising children as well as being obedient to their husbands.

These traditional views are not the only choices, however. Jane Smith, a scholar on Islam presents a more open view in her essay "Islam" in the book *Women in World Religions:* "The new Islamic woman . . . is morally and religiously conservative and affirms the absolute value of the true Islamic system for human relationships." This new Muslim woman disagrees with an interpretation of Islam that oppresses women. She is quite open to educational and professional advancement for herself, though she may think some professions are more appropriate for women than others. Additionally, she does not mind extending sole decision-making power to a male member of her family in certain circumstances in return for security.

In reality, today's American Muslim female community is a mix of all these models: educated and uneducated, married and unmarried, liberal and conservative, as diverse a population as American women in general. For example, I am educated, do not wear *hijab*, expect to have a career, a good marriage (possibly arranged), and kids. You're probably thinking that those expectations are not all that different from those of the average American woman, with the exception of the *hijab* and arranged marriage.

For many Muslim girls, arranged marriage or semi-arranged to someone your parents introduced to you is no more odd than dating and marrying one of your older brother's friends, or someone you met at work. The same is true of *hijab*. Muslims have been exposed to these traditional aspects of Islam for most of their lives.

American Muslim women are really between two worlds: the old world of traditions, preserved and passed down by immigrant parents or older members of the indigenous community, and the new world, as presented to us by the feminist movement, American emphasis on gender equality, and by the Qur'an, in a sense, too.

Women's Rights in Islam

The idea of a Muslim feminist strikes Americans as odd. American Muslim women are in the unique and paradoxical position of living in a society where they are free to explore their religion but are stereotyped by the greater population of their country as oppressed. The West cites its perceptions of arranged marriages, polygamy (actually polygyny, meaning a plurality of wives), veiling, and other aspects of Islamic life that are perceived to degrade women as evidence of Islam's cultural inferiority.

At the same time as they encounter this criticism, American Muslim women are rediscovering the freedoms Islam gives them. Muslims believe that God revealed to Prophet Muhammad several provisions emphasizing a woman's independence, provisions which are recorded in the Qur'an. Of particular note is that in the Qur'an Eve is created independently of Adam, providing no Qur'anic basis for women's existence as the result of the creation of men.

In the Qur'an, men and women are fully equal before God. Marriage is a contract to be negotiated, even to the woman's benefit, and women have the right to divorce, one of many Qur'anic "innovations" that "brought legal advantages for women quite unknown in corresponding areas of the Western Christian world," says Jane Smith. Other innovations include the right to own property and the right to inherit money. According to Islamic law, a woman can keep her maiden name and her personal income. Islam also grants women the right to participate in political affairs and vote (imagine, if we had all followed the Qur'an, there would have been no need for the suffragette movement), to stand equally with men in the eyes of the law, to receive child support in the event of a divorce, to seek employment and education, to accept or turn down a marriage proposal, and to live free from spousal abuse. Islam also gives women high status as mothers, to be respected and admired by their children. On two occasions the Prophet highlighted the mother's role, telling one follower to stay with his mother rather than join the military, "for Paradise is at her feet." Muslim women also can draw on a history of strong women, particularly those who lived in Muhammad's time. Some Muslims even support a woman's right to abortion because the procedure is believed to have been performed in the Prophet's time without his dissent. . . .

A New Examination of Islamic Theology

Muslim women . . . can improve their situation by taking advantage of the opportunities a Muslim woman has in America. Living in the United States is positively affecting the lives of American Muslim women in two ways: (1) American culture encourages female participation in religious activities; and (2) Muslim women are readily able to learn Arabic, read the Qur'an, and analyze the Qur'an for themselves.

One of the greatest phenomena occurring in the Muslim world today is Qur'anic exegesis by Muslim feminists. The Qur'an, a book regarded as the divine word for over 1400 years, is being interpreted from a non-male perspective on a large scale for *the first time ever*. A diverse group of the world's female Muslims are "fundamentally [reworking Islam] . . . from a feminist and egalitarian point of view," [as Barbara Crossette reports in the *New York Times*]. Their work is controversial because they are trying to prove that the Qur'an does not support oppression of women without undermining or questioning the validity of the Qur'an itself, only certain interpretations. Some credit the Beijing United Nations Conference on women for bringing this intellectual, yet politically charged, dialogue to the surface, and now the Ford Foundation, the National Endowment for Democracy, and the Council on Foreign Relations are funding projects in this area.

I say it's about time. For 1400 years, men like my grandfather have told women like me what the Qur'an says. I'm not saying all those men are wrong. And frankly, the only interpretations I'm really interested in challenging are the ones regarding women's so-called inferiority. I'm just saying that, now that women have an opportunity to be literate, to read the Qur'an in Arabic, and tell us if they think God made men superior, let's have a listen!

The core complaint of these feminist Muslim theologians is that though the Qur'an is clear in its support of women's rights, men have been interpreting the Qur'an to their own advantage since its revelation. Amina Wadud-Muhsin, philosophy and religion professor at Virginia Commonwealth University in Richmond, says, "Now . . . many women are making the point that . . . men's interpretation of our religion . . . has limited women's progress, not our religion itself." For example, the gender segregation during prayer now suggests inferiority on women's part when, in actuality, the Prophet initiated the practice so that women would not have to prostrate in front of men. Realizing that a male perception of Islam has been used and accepted for centuries, Muslim women are taking back their right to Qur'anic education and interpretation.

The movement is part of an Islamic renaissance worldwide that gives Muslim women the opportunity to study Islam. Critics of the movement, orthodox and mainstream Muslims, claim that it is yet another tactic to discredit Islam. But Muslim theologian and religion professor Rifaat Hassan at the University of Louisville believes that "What we are witnessing today is the beginning of one of Islam's greatest revolutions, the women's revolution." Feminist scholars like Hassan feel they are strengthening Islam against the standard Western criticisms of female oppression.

For example, American Muslim men are trying their best to explain *Surah* [Qur'anic chapter] 2:228 and 4:34, passages emphasizing men's superiority. The dominant translation of 4:34, one handed down over centuries, advocates hitting one's wife *lightly* in *extreme* cases. A.J. Arberry's translation reads, "And those you fear may be rebellious admonish; banish them to their couches, and beat them." Kamran Memon says of this troublesome passage in his article "Wife Abuse in the Muslim Community":

> Tragically, some Muslim men actually use Islam to "justify" their abusive behavior. Focusing on rituals, considering themselves to be Islamically knowledgeable, and disregarding the

spirit of Islam, they wrongly use the Qur'anic verse that says men are the protectors and maintainers of women to go on power trips, demand total obedience, and order their wives around. They disregard the Islamic requirement for the head of the household to consult with other members of the family when making decisions. Then, if their wives dare to speak up or question their orders, these men misinterpret a Qur'anic verse that talks about how to treat a disobedient wife and use it as a license for abuse.

Muslim women are reinterpreting the texts for themselves and pointing out alternate, less controversial, and possibly more accurate interpretations. The usual explanation, which Memon cites, of the more offensive translation (including the instructions to beat) is that men, in Islam, have the large burden of keeping their houses in order and must carry out their responsibilities as they see fit. Hassan's analysis gives a different perspective:

The first point to be noted is that it [the Qur'anic passage that is interpreted to advocate beating] is addressed to *ar-rijal* ("the men") and to *an-nisaa* ("the women"). In other words, it is addressed to all men and women of the Islamic community. . . . Here, it is important to point out that the Arabic word that is generally translated as "beating," when used in a legal context as it is here, means "holding in confinement," according to the authoritative lexicon *Taj al-'Arus.* . . . I have analyzed sura 4, verse 34 in order to show how the words of the Qur'an have been mistranslated in order to make men the masters and women the slaves.

Though not all American Muslim women can be scholars like Hassan, they can benefit from the American tradition of women participating in church activities every Sunday. Women participate in and run fundraising activities, and they attend the Sunday service as well as teach Sunday School.

American ideals have influenced Islamic religious practice in those two ways: women are recognized as suitable teachers, and activities are held on the American holy day, Sunday. Immigrant women's participation in the mosque is definitely greater in the United States than in most of the Islamic world. For both immigrants and American-born women, participating in mosque activities can be empowering when they take the opportunity. If it weren't for American culture that emphasized Sundays as a gathering day for everyone in the family, American Muslim women might never have gained leadership roles in the mosque. In this case, American culture has trumped chauvinistic immigrant culture. . . .

Many opportunities for American Muslim women to unify as a

group are occurring today. With more young Muslim women attending college, they will interact with a variety of Muslim women (and men) and perhaps learn to function as a group of American Muslim women and not as representatives of their culture only.

In addition, as the shortage of men within a particular ethnic group continues, a fact true for both Palestinians and African-Americans, young women with their mothers' blessings will sacrifice a shared heritage with their spouse for shared religion with their spouse, as it should be in America. Ethnic groups will be less clannish as more interethnic marriages take place, leading to interethnic unity and support among Muslim women.

Already, American Muslim women born to immigrant families call themselves feminists, and their families do not reject, in fact accept, them for their views. Perhaps someday, mothers may even see higher education as more than bait for a suitable husband but as a means of empowerment and improvement for their daughters.

A small minority of American Muslims say Americanization and the mixing of the sexes among American Muslims will come to an end, that the progress Muslim women have made will cease as American Muslims become even more conservative. I believe that view is incorrect.

The Islamic principles of ethnic and gender equality are being tested in America, and the combination of American activism and women's liberation according to the Qur'an will continue to bring American Muslim women together. From the emotionally and intellectually charged debate over *hijab* to a suburban Muslim family contemplating a proposal of arranged marriage, the choices of Muslim women will serve as a barometer of Islam's future in America, and the signs are, in many respects, highly promising.

WOMEN AND THE MUSLIM AMERICAN FAMILY

Jane I. Smith

Jane I. Smith is a professor of Islamic studies and the codirector of the Duncan Black Macdonald Center for the Study of Islam and Christian-Muslim Relations at Hartford Seminary in Hartford, Connecticut. In the following passage from her book *Islam in America*, Smith discusses contemporary thinking about the rights and roles of Muslim American women in the home, the workplace, and the school. The family is the central component of Islamic culture, she writes, and therefore Muslim American women usually place the well-being of their families above all else. However, Smith notes, Muslim American women are increasingly trying to juggle the added responsibilities of school and work along with their family obligations. Smith examines a number of issues facing Muslim women in America, including marriage, divorce, child rearing, and domestic violence.

Some observers of Islam in the international arena have predicted that issues involving Muslim women's roles and identities will be near the top of the concerns to which contemporary Muslims must pay serious attention in the coming decades. Certainly, movements for women's rights and for reform of traditional family laws are taking place in many parts of the world. In this as in other areas of Islamic change, America may well prove to be a place both of experimentation and of affirmation of many traditional values. Women and men in the United States are turning their attention increasingly to the ways in which women contribute to the formulation of American Islam as they participate in the public as well as private spheres of Muslim life and are active in academia, various aspects of professional life, and the American workplace. . . .

In the interconnected set of concerns daily facing American Muslims, few issues are more central than those dealing with the family. For immigrants and African Americans alike, maintaining strong family ties is of such crucial importance that much else is, of necessity, secondary. The question of whether women should work, for example, either in full-time professional positions or in part-time jobs to help with family finances, is often framed in terms of how such employment can be balanced with family responsibilities.

The Roles and Responsibilities of Women

Educated American Muslim women are increasingly vocal in their insistence that Islam provides for equal rights and opportunities for women and men, although their roles are to be seen as complementary rather than identical. In some cases, this complementarity may also involve separation of the sexes in the public sphere. It is evident, for example, in the fairly common practice of men and women being separated in worship, meetings, and other public gatherings. While maintaining different space is certainly not mandatory, and many Muslims do not observe it, for others it signifies that women have as much right to define their own space as do men and that they are comfortable sitting and interacting with one another. For many women, it certainly does not curtail their vocal participation in public forums and discussions. "This is not forced segregation," commented a participant in a regional conference on women in New England in 1997. "Often we just feel more comfortable being able to relax with our friends, not worry if our knees happen to touch those of the man next to us, and enjoy a time of comradeship and even a little friendly gossip. Besides, if we object to what is being said we can do it as a block, or in small groups." Many other Muslim women and men, while supporting the complementarity of roles, see little point in not having a free mixing of men and women in most public arenas, although not in worship. . . .

Muslims generally defend few verses in the Qur'an that non-Muslims (especially, perhaps, Western feminists) say indicate the inferior status of women as needing to be seen in context. Women inherit only half of what men inherit, for example, and the testimony of two women is required to equal that of one man in a court of law. These injunctions are interpreted as viable because of the Muslim man's responsibility to take care of and provide for the woman. Many Muslim men and women argue that equity is probably a better term than equality in comparing expectations for men and women and that the distinctions between men's and women's roles and the resulting differences in some of the responsibilities do not mean that one is better or more privileged than the other. Some more progressive voices can be heard saying that some of these passages suggesting what appears to be an inferior status for women must be reinterpreted in the light of new contexts and new roles for women. The one male prerogative that is generally not challenged is that of serving as imam, or religious leader, of a worshiping Muslim congregation. The reason classically cited, and still supported, for women's disqualification is menstruation, which renders her impure and thus unfit to lead the prayer.

Women normally do not participate in religious activities, including fasting during the month of Ramadan, while menstruating.

Balancing Work and Family

Increasingly, both women and men are insisting that women play a dynamic part in shaping American Islam. Even women with families are encouraged to find ways to participate and not use the excuse of responsibilities in the home, which of course must not be ignored, to avoid their communal obligations. While there is little disagreement that Muslim women are allowed to have full professional lives (most American Muslims acknowledge and lament that women in some Muslim countries are still denied these opportunities), there is much discussion about what kinds of professions are appropriate and what family sacrifices, if any, should be made to allow a woman to maintain a full-time job. Many immigrant women note how much more difficult it is to work full-time in the United States because here they do not have an extended family to help care for children. Reluctant to leave their children at a day-care center, many women choose to stay home with them while they are young to provide the family environment and support they feel is crucial in their developing years. When asked if they would be more willing to use day care if it were run by Muslims "in an Islamic way," many say yes, while others still feel that being at home with their young children is essential. Some professional women are willing to risk becoming dated in their fields of expertise, even jeopardizing their professional reentry, rather than leave their children to the care of non-family members.

Other women, however, argue strongly that this willingness on the part of some to sacrifice their careers for the sake of their children is a kind of capitulation to the traditional roles that will keep American Muslims from being full participants in society. What they need to work for, they insist, is the development of cooperative resources among Muslims to provide for child care and the recognition that survival in American society means not retreat but courageous participation. Others disagree strongly. "It seems to me that we can well learn from other American women who have tried the highly professional route and found it just doesn't work with family responsibilities," says a young Egyptian woman. "Divorce rates rise, children get into trouble, and the model of an alternative family structure that true Islam provides gets shattered."

There is little disagreement among American Muslims about the importance of adequate education for girls and women. As they often cite, that the first word revealed by God to Prophet Muhammad was *read* (or *recite*) indicates that all Muslims, women as well as men, must be as well educated as possible. One argument is that part of a woman's religious responsibility is to accept the challenge to expand her knowledge, and God will ask her on the day of judgment why she did not take advantage of all the opportunities available to learn. Another is that if women do not educate themselves, un-Islamic sexist and repressive customs will be allowed to continue. Implied is the assumption that what men will not do for women in terms of reform must come from their own initiative. Both women and men insist that a mother be able to educate her own children intelligently, that an educated woman is necessary for *da'wa*, or calling others to follow Islam (many underscore their conviction that the best person to give the message of Islam to a non-Muslim woman is a woman), and that women be able to participate intelligently in the mutual consultation that is the ideal Islamic way of governing the community. Arguments about what subjects may be appropriate for women to study are still occurring in many parts of the world but do not seem to be a high priority among American Muslims.

The Debate over Proper Attire

One of the most controversial subjects in the American Islamic community is that of appropriate dress for women. Clearly, this is a topic about which many women feel strongly, one way or the other, and about which they are interested in coming to their own determination, apart from the discourse of Western feminism or secular critique. On two important points there is agreement. First, that it is appropriate for both men and women, as the Qur'an itself makes clear, to dress modestly. The issue, of course, is what constitutes modesty. (The Qur'an, despite what some Muslim women seem to think, does not actually specify exactly how much of the body has to be covered.) Second, that the choice of how to dress is completely the woman's and cannot, or at least should not, be forced on her by her father, husband, or any other male relative. For Muslims in many parts of the world, and especially those in America, what is referred to as "Islamic dress" is not necessarily the same as the traditional dress that women from other cultures may have worn. What is now being called appropriately conservative clothing really began to appear after 1967, the time of the Arab-Israeli War, which was seen as so devastating to the Muslim cause. Political observers have noted that defeat brought about much Muslim introspection as to what it means to live Islamically, to assure victory and success under God's guidance. Many women began to wear the *hijab* (head covering) after that time as a sign of their allegiance to Islam, and it soon became one of the manifestations of the Islamic revival that has occurred in so many parts of the world.

The main issue for American Muslims is whether all women must dress conservatively, or Islamically, to be considered good Muslims, and what, in fact, exactly constitutes such dress. African Americans and some Anglo converts are often the most consistent in wearing clothing that covers everything except their hands and face, as well as some kind of head covering. A few choose to wear the full face veil.

That there is now a burgeoning number of stores and retail houses specializing in Islamic dress, including robes (sometimes called *jilbabs*), scarves, and other kinds of fancier headgear and even matching shoes, is a joy for many women and a worry for others. When the dress business begins to sound more like high fashion, some feel due cause for concern.

Many Muslim circles engage in a quite lively discussion about the role of Islamic dress in the success, or lack of it, of women in the workplace. Many women insist that having adopted conservative clothing, they now feel free to enter fully into public life, secure in the knowledge that people will respect them as women of faith and piety. Some even argue that dressing Islamically makes it easier to move up in one's professional field. Many, however, cite the opposite experience. "When I was up for promotion," says a middle-aged Palestinian woman, "my boss called me in and said candidly that because of the public relations aspects of the new position it would be much better if I did not have to wear what he called 'that hat' all the time. I replied that the 'hat' was more important to me than the promotion, and I was not surprised when I didn't get it." Some cite more blatant examples of prejudice, such as women wearing *hijab* to work being called "ragheads" or "mops." If such incidents give pause to some professional Muslim women, they seem to energize others to be even more intentional about their dress. Clearly, the main issue concerning dress has not to do with long sleeves or having one's legs more or less covered. It centers on the headdress that ensures no hair is showing. Hair traditionally has been considered a woman's most alluring aspect, to be revealed only to her husband or immediate family. . . .

Marriage

Marriage is of great importance in Islam, so much so that traditional societies have not had a place for the unmarried man or woman. Muslim families have given great importance to the preparation of daughters for marriage. That importance is naturally changing a bit in the West, although the concern for marriage and family remains paramount.

By Islamic legal stipulation, Muslim men are free to marry Jews and Christians, on the understanding that the male head of the household determines the religion in which the children will be brought up. Muslim women, on the other hand, are not permitted by law and custom to marry anyone but another Muslim, even though the Qur'an does not specify it in quite that way. This freedom of choice for men and not for women has caused some difficulties in American culture, in which Muslims are so much the minority. When young men have chosen to marry outside the faith, women have sometimes found their choice of a marriage partner to be seriously curtailed. In some circumstances, families of eligible young Muslim women have had to look to their home countries to find suitable husbands.

While in America it is not unusual for a Muslim to marry a non-Muslim, pressures are strong for both men and women to choose a partner from within the Islamic community. The conviction of many families that they do not want their daughters to date stems not only from a desire to protect them but from the fear that dating will inevitably lead to greater instances of intermarriage. Often, the additional desire that young people marry within their particular ethnic or cultural group further complicates the marriage issue. Some Anglo Americans who have converted to Islam, for example, are frustrated in their attempts to marry immigrant Muslim women because their families will not permit it. On the whole, African American, Hispanic, and other ethnic minority Muslims tend to marry within their own groups.

It is not unusual for a non-Muslim woman who has married into a Muslim family to feel some pressure to convert, even though it is not legally necessary for her to do so. Sometimes a woman adopts Islam with the hope of relating more easily to her husband's family. Or for her own personal reasons she may choose to become Muslim. The problems are significant no matter what choice a young wife makes and contribute to feelings on the part of both Muslims and non-Muslims that interfaith marriages should probably be avoided if possible and entered into only with the greatest of caution and forethought. . . .

Husbands and Wives

Traditional relationships between men and women in the family structure are under a great deal of scrutiny in America. One of the most highly debated verses in the Qur'an is Sura 4:34, often cited to affirm male authority: "Men have authority over women, because God made the one of them to excel the other, and because they spend of their property [for the support of women]. So good women are obedient. . . . As for those from whom you fear insubordination, admonish them and banish them to beds apart, and beat them."

As the verse makes clear, Muslim men have traditionally been financially responsible for women. Thus, either her husband or some other male relative must take care of a woman's needs. At least in theory, this custom assures that a woman will always be taken care of, and Muslims are eager to point out that the American reality of so many single women, and single mothers, living below the poverty level with no men to support them would be inconceivable in a true Islamic system. The rub is, this financial responsibility means that final decision-making lies with the man. Many Muslim women who think about the matter seriously, even in the American context, consider that this is a small price to pay for security. A young Egyptian woman was asked by an American friend, "Doesn't it really annoy you to think that your future husband will have the last word?" "Yes," said the Muslim girl, "it is frustrating. But I honestly think that if you don't make it a big deal, it is finally the only system that works." But many contemporary Muslims, especially those raised or educated in the American context, are challenging the question of final authority. "Muslims are simply having to figure out new kinds of interpretations that respect the intention of the Qur'anic text but allow for the kind of give and take that Western women generally insist on. And the fact is that in most Muslim marriages today, whatever lip service is given to male authority, the woman knows exactly how to exert power, as she has always known."[1]

It must be said that although "beating" seems to be allowable in the last part of this Qur'anic passage, no reputable Muslim interpreters would suggest that it should involve anything more than the lightest of taps as a reminder to the wife of her conjugal responsibilities. Never can this legitimately be cited as justification for wife-beating, although Muslim men, like Christian and other men, have on occasion resorted to such measures. Domestic violence has been very little discussed in the American Muslim community until recently. Now there is more public recognition that domestic violence in Muslim families is on the rise, although Muslims profess that they are less culpable than their non-Muslim neighbors. Articles in Muslim journals encourage their readers to face the reality of increasing violence, understand the stress factors that contribute to it, and work for its elimination. "Only a strong Islamic character, that condemns anger and emphasizes tolerance and compassion," writes one journalist pleading for Muslim attention to this potential problem, "can reduce the tendency toward violence.". . .

Divorce

American Muslims are also paying more attention to the matter of divorce. They are quick to note that while Muslims are often accused of "easy divorce," in fact, statistics among Muslims worldwide show a much lower rate than among Western Christians. Nonetheless, the fact that many men in the history of Islam have rid themselves of unwanted marriages by uttering what is called the triple *talaq*, or divorce, has without question been an affliction for many women. While considered a reprehensible practice, it has been possible for a husband simply to say three times in a row, "I divorce you, I divorce you, I divorce you." According to Islamic law, practices are not just required or forbidden but fall into grades of acceptability and nonacceptability. This "triple divorce," while historically common, is legally barely acceptable. American Muslims are quick to point out that Prophet Muhammad deemed divorce in any case to be the worst of solutions, to be avoided at almost any cost. If one absolutely must

1. from a conversation among Christian and Muslim women at Harvard Divinity School in the late 1980s

divorce, the process should be carried out over a three-month period according to the more acceptable Islamic legal determination. This is both to make sure that the woman is not pregnant and, giving the man a chance to reconsider his decision, to avoid the possibility of severing a marriage because of the anger of the moment.

The question is often asked whether the husband must initiate the divorce or if a wife, who for whatever reason cannot stand living with her husband anymore, can initiate divorce proceedings. While the system may seem to favor the man, who can divorce at will although certainly not with license, a woman does have recourse in the termination of a marriage if there is good reason. The problem for many women, especially those who are not educated, is that they simply do not know their rights. In many Muslim countries, helping women understand their legal prerogatives has been identified as an important task. Another deeply problematic matter for divorced women in many cultures has been the fate of children of divorced couples. The four major schools of Islamic law, while differing on the age of the child, give custody of both sons and daughters to the father. Like everything else, however, these stipulations are subject to the modifications of American civil law and are often interpreted differently in the Western context.

Children and Youth

As is true of Muslim cultures across the world, having children is a matter of great importance to Muslims living in America. While certain realities, such as the employment of the wife, may place constraints on the number of children a couple will decide to have, to be childless or even to have only one child is often considered a deep disappointment to the larger family. Children are very much a part of the family activities from birth and accompany their parents outside as well as inside the home as often as possible. At most social occasions, in the women's section of the mosque, or even in group meetings and conferences, children are present and occupy themselves playing around their mothers. Muslims use babysitters only when they absolutely have to, believing that the more children are with them the better they will understand, and feel a part of, community events. The occasional disruptions caused by children's squabbling, crying, or making demands on their parents are generally seen as normal and perfectly acceptable. On the whole, Muslim children are well behaved and learn at an early age how to amuse themselves in public and social gatherings that may keep them up past their usual bedtime.

How to raise children in American society and culture is an ongoing concern to all Muslim parents. Deeply worried about the influences of American television, for example, many families have strict rules for the number and kind of shows their children may watch and try to find acceptable alternatives. Many parents take advantage of the huge amount of material that is now available through various Muslim agencies for helping children focus on wholesome issues in the context of an Islamic identity. They buy videos in which puppet characters like Adam, dressed in Muslim garb, talk to young children about how happy he is to be a Muslim, how lovely a trip to the Ka'ba in Mecca can be, and how Allah should be thanked for all the good things of life. An Arabic Playhouse video teaches children the stories of the Qur'an. Muslim Scouts Adventures substitute for the often violence-filled cartoons of American TV, and heroes of Islamic history such as Fatih, in the story of Sultan Muhammad II, capture their imagination. Tapes like "Alif [the first letter in the Arabic alphabet] is for Asad [lion]" provide early lessons in Arabic. Designed for young readers, *Young Muslim* magazine (published by Sound Vision) features stories, puzzles, comics, and interviews with well-known Muslims such as Muhammad Ali and Hakeem Olajuwon.

Many Muslim parents discuss with one another ways to reinforce Islamic identity in their young children and teenagers. Interaction with non-Muslim children and youth is both inevitable and, in the view of most Muslims, a good thing. But it can lead to difficulties if the young people of the community do not possess the tools to help them understand their differences and see them as a matter of personal pride and significance. As children reach the teenage years, issues of identity often become more complicated for young Muslims. Sometimes they may feel some pressure to live double lives. Comfortable with their Muslim identity at home, and at least reasonably willing to conform to the expectations of their elders while with relatives, they may find it tempting to drop that identity in the more public aspects of their lives, especially as they socialize with friends who are not Muslim. Some girls may even leave home wearing Islamic head covering with the intention of removing it later. Muslim journals are eager to report the testimonies of young women who insist that they find the *hijab* a source of pride and distinction when they do wear it to school. . . .

These, then, are some of the concerns that face Muslims in America as they ponder the rights and roles of women, work for the establishment and maintenance of sound family structures, and struggle to raise and support their children.

THE MARRIAGE CHALLENGE FOR SINGLE MUSLIM CAREER WOMEN

Munira Lekovic Ezzeldine

In the following article, writer Munira Lekovic Ezzeldine argues that American Muslim women receive mixed and often contradictory cultural signals regarding their roles. As youths, Ezzeldine says, American Muslim girls are encouraged to pursue their education as well as any career goals to which they may aspire. Ezzeldine goes on to say that once American Muslim women reach adulthood, however, their families and peers put a greater emphasis on the importance of marriage and domestic life, often at the expense of professional ambitions. Ezzeldine addresses the fear that hard-fought successes in educational and career opportunities will still be discounted by family and religious traditions that have historically emphasized a woman's role in the home as wife and mother. Ezzeldine is the author of *Before the Wedding: 150 Questions for Muslims to Ask Before Getting Married.*

My husband and I recently tried to match-make a couple of our friends. Omar began telling his friend about a really nice woman we knew at 33, successful, beautiful. His first response was, "So, what's wrong with her? Why is she 33 and not married?" Looking at the 30-year-old man before me, my first thought was, "I could ask you the same thing." However, the reality set in that there's a double standard when it comes to the issue of age and marriage.

Success or Spouse?

Many Muslim women are successful lawyers, doctors, professors and journalists. They are outspoken and active in their Muslim and non-Muslim communities. They are intelligent and beautiful, and they are unmarried. The same women who are ambitious and focused on their academic and professional success are finding it difficult to find a suitable spouse.

Twenty years ago, as young Muslim boys and girls were being raised in the U.S., they were encouraged to excel academically and professionally. Parents placed a huge emphasis on education and hard work for both boys and girls. And apparently, they were taken seriously. Girls excelled and never felt they could not attain an education or a profession. They worked hard and succeeded as their parents had encouraged all those years. Now, these same women are in their twenties and thirties and the same parents are now pressuring them to get married.

Are women to blame for being ambitious and educated? Apparently so. Women seem to be penalized for their ambition. Once a young woman passes the age of 25 and remains single, she is considered "old" and often finds it difficult to find a suitable spouse.

Suddenly, others tell her that she has become too picky and her expectations of a husband are unrealistic and that she should hurry up and get married already. "There are some of us who went to college and are successful in our careers and we are not on a search and destroy mission to get married," says Suhad Obeidi, a 39-year-old former banking manager with an M.B.A. The reality is that Muslim women have worked hard for their education and careers and they will not give it all up in order to get married.

Traditional Roles

In recent decades, men have also become highly educated and progressive, and have even fought for women's rights and the elevation of women in Islam. However, while these men are impressed with a successful and active woman, they do not consider her "marriage material." Despite the elevation of women, many men have maintained traditional ideas as to the type of wife they seek. After all, they do not see anything wrong with the way their mother was.

Consciously or subconsciously, many men seek a wife who will fulfill the traditional role of a wife and mother and one who will maintain a traditional home life. She should be educated, but she should also be willing to put her education and career on a shelf while raising a family. These women in their late twenties and early thirties appear too established in their career and lifestyle and therefore, more difficult to marry because they will not fall into this traditional role.

Many American Muslim women want to be wives and mothers while at the same time be respected for their profession. "One big problem is that, rather than embrace her ambition and success, men simply tolerate it and expect something in return," says Nagwa Ibrahim, a 25-year-old activist seeking a career as a human and civil rights lawyer.

The Example of Khadija

Current expectations of marriage have changed for women and become more aligned with the examples of women during Prophet Muhammad's lifetime. The Prophet's first wife, Khadija, was an established career woman who was 15 years older than her husband.

Khadija was a very confident and successful woman who actually proposed to the 24-year-old Muhammad. Yet, the Prophet was not intimidated by her nor found her "unmarriageable."

They maintained a strong marriage as she continued to be a busi-
nesswoman, as well as wife and mother. Prophet Muhammad and
Khadija were married for 28 years, the longest of all his marriages. The
year that Khadija died was also referred to as the Year of Mourning by
Prophet Muhammad.

Many Muslim women seek not to compete with men, but rather to
establish a partnership with their spouse. Ultimately, these women
want to be cherished and loved in the same way that the Prophet
loved Khadija. This type of partnership in marriage can only exist
when both people are accepting and respectful of one another's ambitions and priorities in life.

Partnership in Marriage

Nagwa Ibrahim feels that men have succumbed to negative cultural
stereotypes that are contrary to Islam when selecting a spouse. "We
(Muslim women) are the way we are because we are trying to be good
Muslims," she says.

Thus, a partnership in marriage can only be developed when men
and women really follow the principles of Islam and learn to communicate their expectations of marriage as well as be understanding of
one another.

Communication is vital to any successful marriage, but now more
than ever, women must feel comfortable in expressing their expectations of marriage to a potential spouse and in return feel that they are
being understood, respected and encouraged.

This evolution will happen once we see more modern examples of
successful Muslim men and women getting married and further benefiting society by their union. Educated Muslim men and woman will
only improve our Muslim communities by expecting the best from
everyone, be they men or woman.

Beginning in the homes, parents need to nurture their children by
encouraging them that they can have both worlds and that they can
be successful in their career and marriage. Muslim women can have a
huge impact on the future by modeling the multi-faceted woman of
Islam to their children.

Therefore, when their daughters grow up, they will aspire to be
women of excellence and ambition. Additionally, when their sons
become men, their expectations and views of a suitable wife will include a partnership with an intelligent and successful Muslim woman.
With further education and communication, men and women can
understand and respect one another's roles in society and in the home,
which will ultimately benefit future generations of Muslims.

AMERICAN MUSLIM WOMEN CAN BE BOTH DEVOUT AND LIBERATED

Miriam Udel Lambert

In the following selection, Miriam Udel Lambert notes that because American Islam is an amalgam of religious beliefs from different countries, cultures, and faiths, it allows Muslim women to explore active roles in society while conforming to their religion. Lambert suggests that women can choose roles for themselves, from housewife to business executive to political activist. Lambert also notes the contributions of converts, who may be new to Islam but have longstanding beliefs about the roles and rights of women in American society. Lambert is a freelance writer based in Cambridge, Massachusetts.

Ilham Hameedduddin, in a loose robe and head scarf, is often mistaken for a foreigner. Although her mother is Indian and her father Arab Indian, Hameedduddin was raised in the United States, attended public schools, and is working toward a BA at Middlesex College in New Jersey. Nevertheless, she says, "Neighbors are surprised I can speak English without an accent. They assume I'm fresh off the boat and I just haven't assimilated yet."

Actually, Hameedduddin doesn't plan to assimilate, at least not as far as her religion is concerned. As a proud American and devout Muslim, she is part of a new, "indigenous" American Muslim generation. Until now, this country's Muslim community has included several subgroups: immigrants from Arab countries and the Indian subcontinent, along with American converts of European or African-American descent. Since immigration restrictions were eased in the late 1960s, many Middle Eastern and South Asian Muslims have come to the States, building a network of mosques and Islamic schools in major metropolitan centers such as Philadelphia and Los Angeles, as well as enclaves in smaller cities like Dearborn, Michigan, and Syracuse, New York, and in smaller towns throughout the country. These developments dovetailed with the growth of the Black Muslim movement, an African-American nationalist religious group founded in Detroit in 1930. (Today a splinter group called Nation of Islam and led by Louis

Farrakhan remains distinct, but the majority of African-American Muslims belong to mainstream Islam.)

Now, according to Georgetown Islamic scholar Yvonne Haddad, the children of these disparate immigrants and converts are in college and graduate school. They are intermarrying with one another, engaging each other socially and religiously, and generally fusing their ranks into a single Islamic community. By virtue of the American context in which this community is emerging—with its emphasis on pluralism and acceptance of difference—it offers women a more public role as workers, activists, and decision makers than most other Islamic societies. Therefore, a new kind of American Islam is being created in which women can be at once devout and publicly active.

The first indication of the openness of American Islam is the way Muslims from different points on the religious and cultural spectrum describe women's religious and communal activities. No matter how religiously liberal or conservative, and regardless of background, all emphasize that Muslim women are engaging in as vast an array of careers and causes as other American women. According to Cynthia Sulaiman, who converted at age 28 after 10 years of deliberation and who now runs the Muslim Homeschooling Resources Network out of her home, "We run just like any other religious community. We have mothers who are strictly stay-at-home and very conservative women who are doctors and scientists, and women who publish magazines for other women. It all depends on what individual women feel they can contribute." She points out that while her community includes many female teachers and health care workers, such professions have been traditional fields for women generally.

Both Devout and Liberated

There are several factors contributing to this new notion of a devout, but liberated, Muslim woman. First, as Muslims of many ethnicities learn to coexist, they have to learn to be open-minded about each other. And people have applied that new tolerance to women as well. Although mosques are sometimes segregated de facto by their location in certain neighborhoods or on college campuses, many serve ethnically, racially, and socioeconomically mixed communities. This is especially true of smaller communities, as Sakina Abdul-Malik points out. While she grew up in Philadelphia in a predominantly African-American mosque, her mosque in Syracuse includes Yemeni, Palestinian, and Malaysian families along with American converts.

In marriage, too, there is much mixing among different Muslims in the United States. Many American-born women are married to Pakistani and Bangladeshi men. According to Haddad, there is a growing rate of intermarriage between Arabs and Pakistanis and between Pakistani men and Bangladeshi women. Meanwhile, all of these families are living in America, rearing children who absorb at least some of the

American ethos. The movement toward inter-Muslim integration in this country, with its prospects for a more public role for women, seems inexorable. "There is a fear of the unknown on the part of parents who believe the more you have someone like you, the happier the marriage is," concedes Haddad. "They absolutely want their children to marry someone from the same country and social class, but the kids aren't paying attention."

A second indicator that American Islam offers new options to women is that young women have taken on a very visible, vocal role as political activists—something that is less common in many Muslim countries. During this election year [2000] in Hameedduddin's community, teenage girls manned a booth outside her local mosque during Friday prayers, urging congregation members to register to vote. During the recent Israeli-Palestinian tensions, women and girls handed out brochures, helped organize protests, and served as spokespeople to the media and non-Muslims. Hameedduddin attributes this activism to the younger generation's greater facility with the English language. Some women choose lesser public engagement, but even they are careful to note that their choice is individual and shouldn't be binding for all Muslim women.

Expressing an attitude typical of many American Muslims, Hameedduddin is deeply respectful of her co-religionists abroad. "In Islamic countries," she points out, "women are much more active among themselves. The 'behind-the-scenes' roles are not lesser roles. Lately, there have been a lot of demonstrations, with women doing a lot of work behind the scenes." If American Muslim women play a more visible role, she argues, it is in the service of achieving their goals effectively: "It's true that women and especially the American youth are much more aggressive in their approach. We've learned new ways to make our voices heard, be active in the community, and draw positive attention to our community. American Muslim women are more assertive than Arab ones because that is simply how American society is set up."

Contributions of Converts

As women become more vocal—more American—they are not straying from their religion, however. Instead, women have brought American activism to their religion. Both scholars and practitioners of the religion are impressed with the enthusiasm that converts often exhibit upon joining the community. Haddad, who has studied American Muslims extensively, notes that female converts take a lot of initiative in establishing religious schools because they are eager for their children to receive a proper Islamic education. Furthermore, they tend to serve as liaisons with non-Muslims because, "they feel themselves to be ambassadors to the larger American society."

Furthermore, novices may insert vigor into their religious commu-

nities. Hameedduddin contrasts those who are born into Islam and
"take it for granted" with a young woman who converted a year and a
half ago and is very good at organizing events in the mosque. "I think
she has brought energy from outside the religion," Hameedduddin
notes. "People like her are more grateful they found [Islam]."

Sulaiman sees the high-profile contributions of converts as a function of practical know-how in dealing with American institutions and
systems rather than as a manifestation of religious passion. Most of the
organizing work in her community in eastern Massachusetts is done
by converts like herself, says Sulaiman, but this is only natural. "I'm in
my native country," she points out, "and I don't expect immigrants to
know what to do in my country. It would be really presumptuous to
walk into a country and say, 'Okay, you have to do this and this.'"
Abdul-Malik, an African-American woman who grew up Muslim in
Philadelphia, echoes her close friend Sulaiman: "Women from overseas
are often homebound, into doing things just with their families. Those
born on this coast are used to doing things in a community."

There are plenty of converts to do that organizing. Muslim Web sites
teem with first-person accounts of "Why I Became Muslim." Many of
the authors are female, as women are among the fastest-growing segments of the Muslim community, according to Ibrahim Hooper of the
Council for American-Islamic Relations. Therefore, it is women who are
helping speed the path to the new American type of Islam.

Oppressive . . . or Liberating?

Though American Muslim women are comfortable with their roles,
many non-Muslim women are mystified by Islam's appeal. They
know that Islam permits polygamy (a controversial practice, though)
and, as it is interpreted in several countries, grossly limits women's
educational and career choices as well as their freedom of movement
and dress.

However, these restrictions are only part of the picture, and a secondary part for the Western women who are choosing the religion. In
her cogent analysis, *Women and Gender in Islam*, Egyptian-born
scholar Laila Ahmed argues that in matters concerning women there
is a dichotomy between the practice of Islam as codified by the legal
tradition and the egalitarian vision portrayed by the Qur'an. She
writes, "The unmistakable presence of an ethical egalitarianism
explains why Muslim women frequently insist, often inexplicably to
non-Muslims, that Islam is not sexist. They hear and read in its sacred
text, justly and legitimately, a different message from that heard by
the makers and enforcers of orthodox, androcentric Islam." When
interpreted directly from the text—rather than when observed in its
most restrictive application—Islam may be understood as egalitarian.

While many Western women consider certain Muslim practices
oppressive, others interpret them liberating. Some women, for exam-

ple, argue that embracing Muslim norms of modesty releases them from the sexual current underlying many everyday interactions. "Islam offers an alternative to a sexually charged and sexually exploitative society," Hooper asserts. "Islam allows women to disengage from an environment that values them only for their sexuality and physical appearance and seeks to eliminate sexuality from non-sexual relationships. If a woman goes to the butcher shop, she doesn't need to look pretty to get meat."

As Muslims negotiate their relationship with American culture—and with Muslims of other ethnicities in the United States—a window has opened for a renegotiated role for women. Taking advantage of that opportunity, women may seek the most egalitarian interpretation of the Qur'an while preserving the traditions they find meaningful. This new role for women may strengthen both women's options and American Islam itself.

CHAPTER 4

AMERICAN MUSLIMS AFTER THE SEPTEMBER 11 ATTACKS

Contemporary Issues
Companion

THE MUSLIM AMERICAN COMMUNITY A YEAR AFTER THE ATTACKS

Riad Z. Abdelkarim

In the following article, Riad Z. Abdelkarim describes the experiences of Muslim Americans during the year after the terrorist attacks of September 11, 2001. The immediate effects of the attacks on the Muslim American community were often negative, Abdelkarim writes, including an increase in suspicion of and violence against American Muslims. However, he relates, there was also an outpouring of support toward the Muslim community. Abdelkarim notes with concern the trend toward governmental policies that he believes are discriminatory, such as the profiling of Muslim Americans by law enforcement and the freezing of the assets of Muslim charitable groups. Muslim Americans need to reach out to their non-Muslim neighbors and to become more politically active, he concludes. Abdelkarim is a physician and a communications director for the Council on American-Islamic Relations.

As our nation approaches the one-year anniversary of the Sept. 11 terrorist attacks, American Muslims around the country will join their fellow citizens in pausing and reflecting upon the horrors of that day and its aftermath. While commemorating the event in their mosques, Islamic centers, and schools, America's estimated six to seven million Muslims also will ponder the aftermath of the attacks on their community—and indeed on the larger issue of Islam in America.

The Initial Response to the Attacks

Muslims were shocked, saddened and outraged at the vicious attack on our own soil—and they did not hesitate to voice their unequivocal condemnation.

In fact, American Muslim and Arab-American organizations and leaders were among the first to react in an organized fashion to condemn the terrorist attacks on that very same day, long before it became clear that individuals calling themselves Muslims were involved in the attacks.

Riad Z. Abdelkarim, "American Muslims and 9/11: A Community Looks Back . . . and to the Future," *Washington Report on Middle East Affairs*, vol. 21, September/October 2002, p. 82. Copyright © 2002 by the American Educational Trust. All rights reserved. Reproduced by permission.

On Sept. 11, 2001, the Council on American-Islamic Relations (CAIR), the nation's largest grassroots American Muslim civil rights and advocacy group, distributed a statement which read: "We condemn in the strongest terms possible what are apparently vicious and cowardly acts of terrorism against innocent civilians. We join with all Americans in calling for the swift apprehension and punishment of the perpetrators. No cause could ever be assisted by such immoral acts. All members of the Muslim community are asked to offer whatever help they can to the victims and their families. Muslim medical professionals should go to the scenes of the attacks to offer aid and comfort to the victims."

CAIR also urged Muslim relief agencies to "offer support in the recovery efforts." Individual Muslims were asked to donate blood and cash.

Similarly, the Muslim Public Affairs Council (MPAC) issued the following unequivocal statement: "We feel that our country, the United States, is under attack. All Americans should stand together to bring the perpetrators to justice. We warn against any generalizations that will only serve to help the criminals and incriminate the innocent. We offer our resources and resolve to help the victims of these intolerable acts, and we pray to God to protect and bless America."

And, in a Sept. 11 letter to President [George W.] Bush, American Muslim leaders stated: "American Muslims, who unequivocally condemned today's terrorist attacks on our nation, call on you to alert fellow citizens to the fact that now is a time for all of us to stand together in the face of this heinous crime." This letter was signed by the leaders of the American Muslim Alliance, the American Muslim Council, CAIR, MPAC, the Muslim American Society, the Islamic Society of North America, the Islamic Circle of North America, the Muslim Alliance in North America, and American Muslims for Jerusalem.

Despite the unanimous and vocal condemnations by American Muslim and Arab-American groups and leaders nationwide, however, some media pundits were not satisfied. In subsequent weeks and months, numerous unsubstantiated references would appear in newspaper opinion columns and on television talk shows about American Muslims' "silence" after the terrorist attacks. Such claims were clearly not based on facts, but rather were the products of either outright ignorance—which is inexcusable—or deliberate defamation—which is utterly deplorable.

The Backlash

Following the initial hours of shock, grief, and anger—when it became apparent that the suspects in the attacks were Arab Muslims—American Muslims and Arab Americans braced themselves for an anticipated vicious backlash.

For American Muslims and Arab Americans, the tragedy that befell our nation was doubly painful. First, like the rest of the country, we watched in stunned horror as the twin towers of the World Trade Center and the Pentagon were attacked. Many wondered whether any friends or loved ones were aboard one of the hijacked planes or inside one of the targeted buildings.

Then, when speculation centered on people of Middle Eastern descent as suspects in these terrible acts, Muslims were forced to turn their attention elsewhere as well. A widespread backlash—borne of misguided rage, ignorance and hate—engulfed the American Muslim and Arab-American communities.

Across the country, there were well over 1,000 reported hate incidents and hate crimes, including murders, arson, vandalism, physical and verbal assaults, and telephoned threats. Muslim women wearing hijab were assaulted, and Muslim children were taunted at school. Mosques, Islamic schools, cultural centers, and Muslim- or Arab-owned businesses from New York to Dallas to California were the targets of death threats, bomb scares, vandalism and assault. A Muslim man of Pakistani origin was shot dead in Texas, while an Indian Sikh gas station attendant who may have been mistaken for a Muslim was gunned down in Mesa, Arizona. So widespread was the fear, many Muslim women stayed indoors, and some Muslim parents did not send their children back to school for days after the attacks.

In those early hours and days after the terrorist attacks, Muslims were comforted to hear words of support for their community by federal, state, and local officials. President George W. Bush's visit to a Washington, DC, Islamic center just a few days after the attacks was a welcome departure from the fledgling administration's previous disinterested stance vis-a-vis the American Muslim community.

Acts of Kindness and Compassion

While there were many documented hate incidents and hate crimes against American Muslims, Arab Americans, South Asians, and others who resembled them (including Mexican Americans and Native Americans), there were also countless acts of compassion, tolerance and friendship. Many of these were not officially documented, but their immeasurable value in boosting the morale of the besieged American Muslim community cannot be overestimated.

These tales truly demonstrated the American spirit of reaching out to those in need. Neighbors volunteered to escort Muslim women to the grocery store. Churches offered their buildings to Muslims for prayer after acts of vandalism and arson. Non-Muslim women symbolically donned the hijab in solidarity with Muslim women. Non-Muslim neighbors of mosques offered to provide security for praying worshippers. Some acts were as simple as a smile to a woman wearing hijab walking on the street.

This overwhelming support was heartwarming and reassuring to a community under siege. Most Americans realize American Muslims and Arab Americans love their country just as much as everybody else and were equally traumatized after the terror attacks.

Interrogations, Detentions, and Profiling

After the initial wave of hate crimes, a second manifestation of the backlash ensued. Sadly, this backlash was in part sanctioned and carried out by our government. FBI agents began to interview tens of thousands of American Muslims and Arab Americans around the country. The manner in which many of these interviews were carried out led community leaders and members to feel that they were being treated as suspects.

These interviews did nothing to further the investigation into the Sept. 11 attacks—not a single Arab American or American Muslim was arrested or charged. Non-citizen student visa or green card holders were in some cases detained—and some deported—for minor visa violations. Rather than assisting the investigation, these heavy-handed FBI and INS tactics contributed to the atmosphere of suspicion and mistrust with which Muslims were being viewed. In addition, the interviews had a chilling effect on the community with many people fearful of speaking out against the subsequent curb on civil liberties or the war in Afghanistan for fear of being labeled "unpatriotic" or "un-American."

Even more serious than these voluntary interviews have been the detentions of hundreds of individuals—mostly non-citizen Arab or Muslim males—by the FBI and INS without charge, without public hearings, without allowing legal representations, and without even revealing their names. These draconian detentions have been the target of widespread. coordinated efforts by civil liberties and Arab-American and American Muslim advocacy groups.

With "profiling" brazenly being conducted at the federal government level, it is no surprise that such actions have been carried out in other settings as well. Hundreds of cases of passenger profiling at airports have been reported. In addition to several highly publicized cases where Muslim- or Arab-appearing passengers were forcibly removed from planes because of passenger or flight crew "discomfort," there have been many more subtle incidents where Muslim passengers have been singled out for extra security screenings and in some cases questioning before being allowed to board airplanes. Most recently, several Muslim passengers were forcibly removed from Greyhound buses in two separate instances.

In addition to the blatant examples of profiling, American Muslims and Arab Americans have been subjected to other, more subtle forms of profiling that are not as easy to prove. Muslims seeking to lease apartments, houses, or commercial spaces have reported repeated rejections from landlords. Anecdotal reports indicate that some Arabs and Muslims, laid off during the economic recession, have found difficulty obtaining employment. The long-term impact of this type of profiling is far greater—both in economic and psychological terms—than the transient humiliation and indignation experienced by profiled airline, train, or bus passengers.

The "War on Terrorism"

American Muslims once again found themselves on the defensive when our nation attacked Afghanistan [in fall 2001]. Generally, American Muslims and Arabs tend to oppose military action in favor of peaceful conflict resolution. In the face of enormous peer pressure by an American public that favored war as a means of seeking revenge on al-Qaeda, however, American Muslim and Arab-American organizations buckled and conformed. Fearful of being labeled unpatriotic—or worse, traitorous—most major American Muslim and Arab-American organizations issued statements of qualified support for the war—along with expressions of concern for the safety of innocent Afghan civilians.

The "war on terrorism" was not limited to overseas foes, but was extended to potential "enemies" at home. The USA PATRIOT Act constituted a major assault on civil liberties in our nation. It was clear to American Muslims that our community was the primary target of this legislation, which gave law enforcement agencies unprecedented powers—and conversely stripped away cherished civil liberties for those unfortunate enough to fall within the wide net it cast—under the guise of "preserving national security" in waging the war on terrorism.

Government Assault on Muslim Charities

American Muslims were still reeling from the post-9/11 backlash, the passage of the PATRIOT Act, and the fallout from the war in Afghanistan when the Bush administration further extended the "war on terrorism" to American Muslim charities. In December [2001] (which corresponded to the Muslim holy month of Ramadan), the government suddenly shut down three American Muslim charities, including the Holy Land Foundation for Relief and Development (HLF—the nation's largest Muslim relief group), Global Relief Foundation, and Benevolence International. The charities all were accused of "funding terrorism" and had their assets frozen—without formal charges being issued against anyone and without any proof brought forward to substantiate the government's claims. . . .

In addition to the direct effects of these closures—the sudden halting in humanitarian assistance to such places as Palestine, Afghanistan, Chechnya, and Kashmir—these closures have had tremendously deleterious indirect effects. Many Muslims are now afraid to contribute donations to any Muslim charity, for fear of being targeted by the FBI for questioning and accusations of "support for terrorism."

Recent comments by a Bush appointee to the U.S. Commission on Civil Rights have added to the feeling among American Muslims and

Arabs that they are being viewed as the "enemy within." At a . . . hearing in Detroit, Commissioner Peter Kirsanow said that "if there's another terrorist attack and if it's from a certain ethnic community or certain ethnicities that the terrorists are from, you can forget about civil rights in this country."

Kirsanow added that another attack could lead to internment camps such as those built to hold Japanese Americans in World War II. "Not too many people will be crying in their beer if there are more detentions, more stops, more profiling," he said. "There will be a groundswell of public opinion to banish civil rights."

Looking Forward: Challenge and Opportunity

Indeed, the past year has been a most difficult one for American Muslims. In addition to the various setbacks detailed above, there have been countless attacks against Islam by conservative commentators, right-wing evangelical Christians, and ardent Zionists. Targets have included virtually every major American Muslim leader and organization, as well as the tenets of the Islamic faith itself, the Qur'an (Muslim holy book), and the Prophet Muhammad himself.

Despite these setbacks, however, American Muslims have much to be proud of. More Americans know more about Islam and Muslims than ever before. Major bookstore chains which previously did not reliably stock even a single copy of the Qur'an now have multiple translations for sale, as well as other thoughtful analyses and treatises by such distinguished scholars as Karen Armstrong, John Esposito, and Akbar Ahmed.

The horrors of the Sept. 11 attacks and the subsequent fallout have resulted in a more rapid maturation of the American Muslim community. Prior to the attacks, one common complaint about Muslims (not without basis) was that we tend to be "insular" and "isolated." Sept. 11 forced American Muslims to emerge from their cocoons of isolation. Finally, Muslims began to reach out to their neighbors and to other faith and ethnic groups. Mosques and Islamic centers around the country began to hold open houses for their non-Muslim neighbors. Muslims have participated in earnest in interfaith gatherings and in town hall meetings with local, state and federal government officials.

On the level of activism and advocacy, American Muslim organizations and leaders have accelerated their involvement and coordination with civil rights groups, and have participated in countless coalitions, panels, and debates. Indeed, American Muslims have stepped forward as the new champions of civil liberties, with other ethnic and civil rights groups looking to them to take the lead in this important struggle.

With respect to Muslim charities, several new humanitarian and relief foundations have formed to fill the voids left by the government-ordered closures of Muslim charities. . . . Essentially, American Muslims are courageously asserting their rights to provide badly needed humanitarian assistance around the world without being intimidated by false accusations and scare tactics.

As for political advocacy, American Muslims have been stung by the realization that their bloc vote for Bush in 2000 did not bring about the anticipated positive effects. Many regret casting their ballot for Bush, while others—particularly community leaders who organized the bloc vote—continue to insist that it was the right decision at the time. In any event, American Muslims have earnestly embarked upon yet another voter-registration drive, now convinced more than ever that they must take it upon themselves to be involved in the process that determines who should represent them. After the trials and tribulations of the past year, even the most skeptical members of the Muslim community have been convinced of the need to register and vote. . . .

The next year post-9/11 will undoubtedly be a challenging one for the American Muslim community—perhaps even more challenging than this first year. With challenge, however, comes opportunity. Nobody really knows what President Bush and Company have planned for the next phase of this "war." One thing is for certain, however: America's seven-million-strong Muslim community—and its leadership—must be ready for any eventuality.

Indeed, along with the millions of other Americans who fear for our country's future, we must be ready to wage a full-scale struggle—a jihad, if you will—for the soul of our nation.

A STATISTICAL PICTURE OF MUSLIM AMERICANS IN THE AFTERMATH OF THE ATTACKS

Dennis Gilbert

Dennis Gilbert is a sociology professor at Hamilton College in Clinton, New York. In this selection, he summarizes the results of a nationwide poll that he and his students developed to gauge the opinions of Muslim Americans following the September 11, 2001, terrorist attacks. According to Gilbert, the survey found that American Muslims had experienced high levels of discrimination and harassment directly after the attacks. However, he adds, the respondents attributed these acts to a prejudiced minority and generally did not perceive non-Muslims as being hostile toward them. The survey also revealed that many American Muslims support U.S. military action in Afghanistan and Iraq even though very few believe that al Qaeda was responsible for the September 11 attacks, Gilbert reports.

The Hamilton College Muslim America Poll is one of the few recent surveys of the Muslim population in the United States. Five hundred twenty-one Muslims over the age of 18 were polled by phone regarding the war on terrorism, related foreign policy issues, and their own experiences of discrimination and harassment. The poll was conducted in April 2002, six months after the shock of the 9-11 attacks, four months after the fall of Taliban in Afghanistan, and three months after President George W. Bush described Saddam Hussein's Iraqi regime as one of three forming an "axis of evil" in the world.

The Muslim America Poll was designed and analyzed by Hamilton College researchers and funded by Hamilton's Arthur Levitt Public Affairs Center. It has a margin of sampling error of plus or minus 5 percent. The survey was conducted in collaboration with the polling firm Zogby International.

The Hamilton poll found an American Muslim population that is largely foreign born, culturally diverse, relatively young, highly edu-

Dennis Gilbert, "The Hamilton College Muslim America Poll: Analysis," May 30, 2002, pp. 4–7. Copyright © 2002 by Dennis Gilbert. Reproduced by permission.

cated, prosperous, family oriented, religiously observant, and inclined toward the Democratic Party.

Seventy percent of respondents were born abroad, though ninety percent are American citizens. *(In this report "American Muslims" refers to the entire national sample, citizen and non-citizen.)* According to the poll, only 38 percent of Muslims in the U.S. are over 45 years old, compared to 52 percent of American adults. Nearly 70 percent of American Muslims over 25 have completed a college education, an achievement they share with just 26 percent of their American peers. Three quarters of Muslim adults, but only half of all U.S. adults are married.

Asked to rate the importance of Islam in their lives, 70 percent chose the top end of a 10-point scale, "extremely important." Eighty percent say they pray daily. Half observe the five daily prayers required of Muslims. Thirty-eight percent of women wear the hair-covering hijab daily or almost daily. With regard to party politics, 36 percent consider themselves Democrats, 18 percent Republicans.

American Muslims reflect the variety of Islamic cultures across the world. One of three respondents to the Hamilton poll was born in an Arabic-speaking country; one in six in Pakistan. Many are African-Americans. Some are black Africans. Six percent are American-born and white. But this impressive cultural diversity appears to have little effect on the opinions of American Muslims. On the issues explored by the poll, differences by ethnicity, citizenship, or for that matter, age and gender, were modest.

Discrimination and Harassment

The Hamilton Muslim America Poll found high levels of anti-Muslim discrimination and harassment, especially in the period after September 11, 2001. However, the poll also revealed that Muslims had encountered widespread expressions of support from non-Muslim Americans.

The poll asked about incidents of "anti-Muslim discrimination, harassment, verbal abuse, or physical attack" directed against "Muslims, Muslim-owned businesses or Islamic institutions" in their communities.

- Sixty percent of the Muslims surveyed reported anti-Muslim incidents in their communities since 9-11. Only 21 percent recalled earlier incidents.
- About half personally knew someone who had been victimized since 9-11.
- One in four respondents had themselves been victims since 9-11.

The incidents reported typically involved "dirty looks," petty harassment, or verbal abuse (sometimes with a menacing edge) in public places. (Airport incidents were surprisingly rare.) A man cuts in front of a Muslim college student, her head covered with a hijab, in a grocery checkout line. He says, "Let Osama's clan wait." A mother and her son are shoved aside by a woman as they emerge from a bank. "Can't you see [us]?" she asks, "I see animals" is the reply. Strangers pull up in front of a Muslim home and scream abuse. A Muslim girl is suspended from school; legal action is required to reinstate her. Another is told she will be blown up.

Although the majority of Muslim American respondents or people they know have been victimized, they did not generally perceive other Americans as hostile. Seventy percent of respondents to the Hamilton poll described Americans as "friendly" or at least "neutral" toward Muslims in the United States. One reason may be the overt support they were receiving from Americans who do not share the attitudes of a bigoted minority. Many respondents said that non-Muslim religious leaders and other prominent people in their communities had publicly condemned anti-Muslim abuses. Seventy percent of American Muslims reported that non-Muslims had "personally conveyed support" to them since 9-11.

Reactions to 9-11 and U.S. Foreign Policy

In early 2002, American Muslims appeared divided and conflicted in their reactions to the September 11, 2001, attacks and their aftermath. Asked if Osama Bin Laden's Al Qaeda network was responsible for the attacks, 44 percent offered no opinion; only a third blamed Al Qaeda. Asked to choose between two alternatives, 40 percent labeled the U.S. worldwide response to 9-11 as a "war on terrorism," but a third saw it as a "war on Islam." Half said they believed that U.S. military action in Afghanistan was justified, 43 percent disagreed.

American Muslims were more unified in their reactions to the widespread questioning and detentions of Muslims in the U.S. by Federal authorities after 9-11: Nearly two-thirds described these actions as "an unwarranted abuse of civil liberties." Only 20 percent said they were "necessary to protect the country from a terrorist threat."

American Muslims share a similar consensus with regard to the Israeli-Palestinian conflict—probably reinforced, during the polling period, by the Israeli invasion of Palestinian territories and the Bush administration's feckless efforts to mediate. Seventy-five percent said they "strongly agree" with the statement "the U.S. has always sided with the Israelis against the Palestinians." Sixty percent rejected the idea that the Bush administration was "trying to bring about a fair peace between Palestinians and Israelis."

By a modest margin (47 to 40 percent), American Muslims agreed that "the U.S. should try to remove Iraqi President Saddam Hussein from power." But they also believed that U.S. economic and military pressure on Iraq were "causing undue suffering for the Iraqi people."

Comparisons between the Hamilton poll and contemporaneous surveys conducted in the U.S. and Muslim countries reveals a pattern of opinion that distinguishes American Muslims from other Americans and from their co-religionists abroad. For example, at the time, 51 percent of the American Muslims polled by Hamilton, close to 90 percent of all Americans in several national polls, but only 9 percent of Muslims in a CNN international survey regarded U.S. military action in Afghanistan as justified. Saddam's removal from power was narrowly favored by American Muslims, supported by a substantial majority of Americans, and overwhelmingly rejected by Muslims abroad. With the exception of the Palestinian question, the American Muslims polled by Hamilton appeared much more divided and ambivalent about foreign policy issues than other Americans or other Muslims. Often their mixed opinions and sympathies suggest a population pulled between two worlds.

America's Muslims Are Beginning to Unite for a Cause

Peter Skerry

In the following article, Peter Skerry explains that Muslim Americans have always been a diverse group, comprised of people of various ethnicities (e.g., Persian, African, Arab, South Asian), national origin (e.g., Egyptian, Syrian, Pakistani, Kurd), and branches of Islam (e.g., Sunni, Shiite, Sufi). These differences have kept American Muslims from developing a unified political coalition, Skerry writes. However, he claims, the terrorist attacks of September 11, 2001, were a defining event for Muslim Americans. After the attacks, Skerry maintains, the U.S. government and non-Muslim citizens began treating American Muslims as a single community. In response, he argues, Muslim Americans are joining together to form a new minority identity. Skerry is a professor of government at Claremont McKenna College in Claremont, California, and a senior fellow at the Brookings Institution.

In the United States today, there is no "Middle Eastern community," no "Arab community" and no "Muslim community," certainly not in any politically cohesive sense.

Muslims and Arabs are a disparate lot, especially in this country. Despite our tendency to equate Arabs with Muslims, the fact is that most Arabs in the United States today are not Muslims—they're Christians from places such as Lebanon. And most Muslims are not Arabs—they're South Asians or African Americans. Muslims here are riven by national, linguistic and sectarian divisions. And many Middle Easterners (Iranians, Turks and Kurds among them) are not Arabs. The divide between Iranians and other Muslim immigrants is particularly telling. Often identifying themselves as "Persians," Iranians in this country have not been highly visible as Muslims. Despite their wealth and great numbers in Southern California, they have built few mosques here. This is now changing. All of these groups are beginning to identify with one another, in no small part because the U.S. government and many citizens are treating them as a more or less homogeneous group. Waging the homeland security battle is necessary. Yet, however one feels about the new Immigration and Natural-ization Service registration requirement for men from many Muslim countries, or about the profiling of Arabs and Muslims more gener-ally, it is important to understand that our policies are helping to forge a new minority identity. We are pushing these groups together into a political coalition around grievances against the government that will not soon be forgotten. The outcome will almost certainly be a new minority group whose claims against America will be a source of rancor and division long after the current crisis has eased.

A Shift in Direction

This shift was evident to me the weekend before Christmas [2002] in Long Beach, Calif., where the Muslim Public Affairs Council (MPAC), a civil rights and ethnic lobbying organization, held its annual con-vention. Founded in 1988, MPAC has since Sept. 11, 2001, emerged as one of a handful of organizations speaking up on behalf of those who perceive themselves to be unfairly targeted by homeland security measures.

This gathering of 1,500 or so offered a vivid display of the variety of Muslims in America. There were Egyptians, Syrians, Lebanese, Palestinians, Pakistanis, Indians, Iranians, Iraqis, Kurds, African Amer-icans and others. There were undergraduates as well as elderly immi-grants. Some spoke Arabic; many did not.

The many women present wore all varieties of dress. A few were in traditional hajibs, heavily covered. Others had full scarves that grace-fully framed their faces. Still others wore small head scarves reminis-cent of those my female relatives wore to Catholic Mass in the 1950s. And some, though modestly dressed, had nothing on their heads and would not have stood out in a crowd—except, perhaps, the stylishly dressed, blonde Palestinian who looked like what she was, the wife of a prosperous Southern California physician.

As sociologist Earle Waugh wrote in the early 1990s, Muslims "may have as much separating them from each other as divides them from the host societies of Canada and the United States." One MPAC leader noted from the podium that there is a pattern of U.S. Muslims from different countries forming separate mosques. But even when this is not the case, as one Pakistani Muslim has observed, "We worship together but then the Pakistanis go back to their curries and the Arabs to their kabobs." Such tendencies reflect not only the influence of diverse ethnic and national cultures on the practice of Islam, but also long-standing sectarian tendencies within the faith, such as those between Sunnis, Shiites and Sufis.

Not surprisingly, such differences have undermined the political cohesion of U.S. Muslims. As religion scholar Kambiz GhaneaBassiri wrote in 1997, "The most important reason why Muslims have not been successful in their political activities is the fact that they rarely

agree on political agendas and are thus unable to form voting blocs."
At the time, GhaneaBassiri also noted: "There is no single problem
confronting the majority of Muslims that would require immediate
organization and effective unifying leadership." Now, of course, there
is just such a "single problem."

The Unifying Problem

The nature of that problem, and its potential to forge an overarching
group consciousness, was evident at the MPAC convention. The event
took place the same week that hundreds of men were arrested in Los
Angeles when they went to meet the new registration deadline. Non-
immigrant males 16 and older from Iran, Iraq, Syria, Libya and Sudan
had to register, be fingerprinted and photographed, and answer questions under oath at their local INS office by Dec. 16. Men from most
other Muslim and Arab countries must register in the coming weeks.
The arrests were for visa and other violations, the INS said, but the
policy has been seen as a trap by many of those called to register.
Among the arrested were Arabs and non-Arabs, Muslims, Christians
and Iranian Jews.

If anything could bring such an agglomeration of individuals from
disparate backgrounds together, it would be just such a government
policy assigning them to the same category and subjecting them and
their families to the intimidating discretion of law enforcement bureau-
crats. A young immigration lawyer, an Iranian-American woman affili-
ated with the National Lawyers Guild, drove the point home to the
gathering: "It's not just an Iranian thing. It's not just an Sudanese
thing. It's not just a Muslim thing." Moreover, the MPAC leaders who
spoke made a point of adding the phrase "American Arabs" whenever
they mentioned "American Muslims."

As charged repeatedly throughout the weekend, the registration
policy is seen as only the most recent in a series, which includes racial
profiling by law enforcement agencies, the investigation of Islamic
charities by the federal government and the secret detention of hundreds of individuals.

Historical Analogies

This of course is not the first time we have targeted groups in the midst
of national crisis. To make sense of today's events, we rely on historical
analogies, yet the ones most widely discussed don't quite work.

Take the persecution of German Americans during World War I,
which led to the virtual elimination of German culture, language and
ethnic identity in the United States. This hardly seems a likely outcome of today's policies, not least because they are far less harsh than
those imposed during World War I, when German language classes
were dropped from school curricula and songs written by Germans
were removed from music books. Today, of course, such policies would

be fiercely fought by advocacy groups such as the American Civil Liberties Union, which was in fact organized in part in reaction to the World War I repression. Not coincidentally, the ACLU was highly visible at the MPAC convention.

The more frequently cited analogy has been with the internment of Japanese Americans during World War II. Yet again, however objectionable today's policies may be, they are simply not as draconian as those experienced by Japanese Americans. And unlike those attending the MPAC conference, Japanese Americans already had a strong group identity at the outset of the war, which had been reinforced by their earlier mistreatment in America. What's going on now is more subtle. Instead of isolating an already cohesive group, we are fostering cohesion where none existed before.

The historical parallel that makes the most sense is one never invoked: that of immigrants from the Italian peninsula who arrived here a century ago identifying themselves as Neapolitans or Sicilians but who gradually came to see themselves as Italians—largely in response to the way they were treated, and mistreated, by Americans. Those Italians were never targeted by government policy the way Arabs and Muslims are today. But that just highlights the greater pressures at work now, when our nation is under attack.

My purpose here is not to debate whether the federal government's current efforts to protect us from our enemies, domestic and foreign, are misguided or inappropriate. Rather it is to warn against discounting or underestimating the anger and panic evident at the MPAC convention and elsewhere.

Such may be the tragic outcome of what is necessary to defend the United States. But if the great social laboratory of America teaches us anything, it is that, in times like these, we Americans demand loyalty of immigrants, and are particularly suspicious of group ties and identities. Our history also teaches that the bonds of ethnic, religious and racial identity that have long characterized our national life get forged in times like these—times when members of minority groups feel vulnerable and threatened.

THE STATE OF ISLAMIC SCHOOLS AFTER THE ATTACKS

Karen Keyworth

Karen Keyworth is an Islamic educator and cofounder of the Islamic Schools' League of America. In this article, Keyworth writes that in the immediate aftermath of the September 11, 2001, terrorist attacks, some commentators accused Islamic schools in the United States of being hotbeds of anti-American Islamic fundamentalism. These critics particularly pointed to the use of textbooks that contained inflammatory, hate-filled material, she explains. According to the author, only a small number of Islamic schools in the United States ever used these textbooks, primarily because they were given to the schools free of charge. Nevertheless, Keyworth asserts, Islamic educators must pay closer attention to the school curriculum to prevent similar occurrences in the future.

An unusual pine tree grows in the American West, the knobcone pine (*Pinus attenuata*)—unusual because it requires searing heat, usually in the form of a brushfire, to open its cone and spread its seeds. The brushfire further benefits the tree by burning away the undergrowth so that when the seeds drop, they will have room to grow. The ash from the fire also helps provide just the right type of soil for these seeds to take root and develop. Too much heat will kill them: too little heat will prevent growth.

The 9-11 attacks on our country were a horrific event that created fear and grief in all Americans. The immediate effects of 9-11 were clear: death, destruction, prejudice, and uncertainty. However, the long-term effects, some of which will be positive, have yet to be fully realized. As with the pine tree, the searing heat that has been brought to bear on the Muslim community initially, and Islamic schools most recently, has the potential to bring growth out of destruction.

Curriculum: The Seeds of Education

The most fundamental area of education in which we seek clarity is the area of curriculum. A school's curriculum is the most divisive,

Karen Keyworth, "Trial by Fire: The State of Islamic Schools After the 9/11 Attacks," *Islamic Horizons*, November/December 2002, pp. 38–42, 44, 52, 54–55, 59. Copyright © 2002 by the Islamic Society of North America. All rights reserved. Reproduced by permission.

most influential, and least understood issue that educators, parents, school boards, and communities must decide. Put simply, a school's curriculum is every academic skill, concept, value, etc. that the school says should be taught to the children and at what level it should be taught. Sometimes these are expressed as benchmarks, guidelines, or student learning outcomes that offer the educator a wide range of ways to make that happen. Sometimes the curriculum is very general: Students will demonstrate appropriate use of punctuation. Other times the curriculum is more detailed: Students will demonstrate appropriate use of capital letters, periods, and commas in a series.

If a curriculum is everything that should be taught, who decides what the curriculum will be? For Islamic schools, the governing boards that usually make this decision frequently choose the curricula for academics from the local school districts, and often the same textbook. This is done for 2 reasons: First, most Islamic schools offer only K–8th grades. Therefore, the students will almost surely attend their local public school, and will need to have studied a similar curriculum if they are to be properly prepared for that school. Secondly, Islamic schools rarely have the financial resources to pay a qualified professional to write a curriculum, one that still might not allow for easy transfer from private to public school. However, this is only a stopgap measure. Muslim children in America require and deserve an education that goes beyond the limited vision of today's typical education.

In an Islamic school that has the time, qualified professionals, desire, and resources, the curriculum (or portions of it) can be very specialized. This is most likely to occur when the school offers all grades K–12. When all levels are offered, there is no need for students to transfer to public school and no need, therefore, to align the curriculum with the local public school. More importantly, Islamic schools that design their own curriculum can go way beyond the typical public school education. They can easily integrate the study of Islam into all aspects of the curriculum to educate students in a way that transforms rather than merely informs—a concept known as *tarbiyah* that is being eagerly embraced Islamic schools across the U.S. and Canada.

The Problem with Curriculum

If curriculum is so simple, why does it create debate within our communities and across the general public? Curriculum has the potential to be divisive because it encompasses all that should be taught—the critical word here is *should*. The word *should* implies that someone will make a judgment based not only on knowledge but also on values.

If we take the example of sex education in the public schools, we can most easily see the role that values play in curriculum decisions. First, there is the decision that educators will teach about sex in the school instead of parents teaching it at home. This demonstrates a value for school being the place where society thinks sex education should occur. Then the decision must be made about what the educators will actually teach—the basics of reproduction, sexually transmitted diseases, safe sex, pregnancy prevention, and/or abstinence? Will the teacher say to the students that they should wait until they are ready to have sex, or that they should wait until they are married to have sex? The curriculum will determine the answer. If curriculum is so loaded with values, why don't parents form a group and just make all the curricular decisions? Parents alone cannot choose curriculum because there is another critical element to deciding curriculum, and that is knowledge of education. Educators have spent years in a classroom learning their profession—first as students and then as teachers. It would not serve our children if we wasted this incredible wealth of knowledge and expertise by removing educators from these decisions. Educators are essential to the process. Obviously, the closer an educator's values and beliefs are to the values and beliefs of the parents, the easier it is to agree on curriculum. Hence, it is imperative that Islamic schools hire Muslim teachers. They can provide that critical combination of professional expertise and knowledge of Islam that a school's curriculum team needs.

Islamic schools, unlike other schools, do not fall into an easily recognizable pattern regarding shared curriculum decision-making. They range from a co-op structure where the parents' role in their children's education is so deep it rivals that of home schooling to the other end of the spectrum, a traditional public school–type where parent teacher organizations (PTO's) are focused primarily on fundraising and not on substantive curricular issues. Each Islamic school is different. The degree to which an Islamic school welcomes and encourages parents to share serious curriculum decisions depends mostly on the principal's professional training and experience. Most university teacher education programs, both in the U.S. and overseas, base their training on a fairly traditional model of education where educators make the most critical curriculum decisions with only minimal input from parents. Most educators are not trained how to integrate parents into curriculum decisions or why doing so is highly desirable. Consequently, it is by accident, not design, when an educator learns to value parents as curriculum partners.

Islamic schools are in a unique position to move away from the dysfunctional traditional public school model to an inclusive model that is more in keeping with Islamic values. As Muslims, we cannot marginalize the God-given role parents are to play in their children's lives. Educators trained within an Islamic education paradigm would already know this.

Islamic Curricula in a Pluralistic Society

Muslim communities across the U.S. are an extraordinarily diverse, exciting and dynamic group. We are American born and immigrant, speak all the major languages of the world, but also vary in the degree of iman, political preference, and ability. It is a challenge to balance a curriculum when students come from widely varying cultures and countries and also live in a country, made up of similarly diverse groups. There is both a strength and weakness in this. Core Islamic values unite us as Muslims, but culture-specific assumptions divide us.

Muslims in America need to balance not only our internal but also external concerns. We have to design a curriculum for Muslim children so that we prepare them to live in America, not elsewhere. According to Dr. Ilyas Ba-Yunus, professor of sociology at SUNY-Cortland, approximately 50 percent of Muslims in America are under the age of 20. They need an education wherein Islam is relevant to and dynamic in their daily lives now as well as in the future. Islamic curricula must actively address real issues in our children's environment. We cannot prepare Muslim-American children for their multiethnic American futures as politicians, media executives, journalists, lawyers, engineers, and more unless we value diversity ourselves. Islam teaches diversity; no other religion is more tolerant or celebrates differences more than Islam. As parents and educators, we should strive to put aside our divisions so that we can create meaningful curricula for our children. If we focus on core Islamic values and teachings, we can do this.

Smoldering Fire or False Alarm?

Regrettably, it is not always a given that educators will focus on core Islamic values and teachings. Some educators indulge themselves by deviating from core values to divisive and extremist values and teachings unacceptable to most Muslims. Although this occurs infrequently, it is highly irresponsible because of the damage it causes to youth and to Muslims in general. In days following 9/11, some sections of the American media have made a play on these fringe textbooks that were being used in a few Islamic schools. Islamic schools have been working on curricular problems for years, so Muslim educators were well aware of the problem of foreign textbooks long before the media discovered them. Unfortunately, because some in the media prefer innuendo to the truth, all Islamic schools are tainted by this situation.

Our internal problem became public when the *Washington Post* produced a piece on Islamic schools that, given the current climate in American society, seemed—and indeed proved to be—inflammatory and misleading. Mixing a little bit of truth with a lot of innuendo and quoting inappropriate sources, the article concluded with sweeping implications that Islamic schools in the nation's capital, and in general, teach hatred. Immediately following this article, and referencing only to it as a source, syndicated columnist Cal Thomas in his article titled "Where Are the Sleeper Cells?" alluded to Islamic schools as terrorist "sleeper cells." Not content with this shocking accusation, he called for Americans to "shut down" these ". . . training grounds of hate currently on American soil." "This is sedition," Thomas sermonized.

This is not sedition. This brouhaha is nonsense, and such tactics are worthy of only the sleaziest in the media. The truth is that a handful of Muslim educators made a serious mistake that is directly related to a lack of funding for Islamic schools across the U.S. Do these textbooks exist? Yes. Do they contain some un-Islamic, hateful teachings? Yes. Do, as Cal Thomas and others imply, Islamic schools across America use them? No.

Islamic schools all across America were initially interested in a free textbook because they needed to save money whenever possible. However, once the objectionable (objectionable to us Muslims, by the way) passages were discovered, the vast majority of schools rejected the texts. In addition to the problems with the content of these books, the way the books presented material was old-fashioned and based on a poor understanding of how children learn. They used "skill and drill" teaching methods that are useful for rote memorization, a technique required for only a tiny portion of a modern Islamic school curriculum.

While there is no excuse for the unprofessional anti-Islamic bias in American media, Muslims must not be intimidated into silence, silence motivated by a need to protect ourselves from further media attacks. We must struggle to keep from behaving like an embattled minority, and we must discuss our problems openly. The vast majority of Muslim educators rejected the hateful texts independently and without knowledge of what other educators thought or were doing. We knew they were not presenting correct Islamic values and teachings. All across America, educators said "NO" to hatred in unison and rejected those texts.

The tiny minority of schools who accepted these texts usually skipped over the objectionable parts when teaching out of them. However, some schools did teach the content of the texts to their students. Whether part of a school's official curriculum or an unauthorized decision by a classroom teacher, the fact remains that students learned this nonsense in school. Let us state unequivocally for all the world to hear that we Muslim educators reject the teaching of hate as completely incompatible with Islam as taught in the Qur'an and the traditions of the Prophet Muhammad. . . . Quite the contrary, the Prophet enjoined peace, tolerance, and moderation.

There is no need to attempt to rationalize this behavior. We should acknowledge our mistakes, correct them, and move on. Even though only a handful of educators actually erred, we all sat quietly by and watched the situation develop. Each of us shares the responsibility for those textbooks ever reaching Muslim students' hands. School boards allowed power struggles to supercede the need to properly fund the schools with quality textbooks. Administrators focused on when teachers arrived to class rather than on what teachers actually taught in class. Teachers allowed themselves to rest in their ignorance, permitting the politically twisted so-called "Islamic teachings" of their youth to go unchallenged and unexplored. Surely common sense would dictate at least a cursory examination of these politically and culturally bound curricula of their countries of origin. Parents soothed their own pangs of guilt for having left their home countries in favor of America by supporting or ignoring this politically motivated rhetoric. Community members focused on acquiring all the material trappings of the American dream instead of strongly supporting their local Islamic school—new cars instead of new texts. We all share in the blame, so we must all share in the solution.

Cal Thomas and other rumormongers can relax. There are no sleeper terrorist cells in Islamic schools, only occasionally sleepy children. Islamic schools are moving away from curricula oftentimes dictated by lack of funds and expertise towards curricula based on sound principals of learning, education, and Islamic knowledge.

Putting Down Roots

The first chance the principal of a new Islamic school might have to look at Islamic studies and Arabic language curricula could be when the delivery person drops a box of books at the school door. Because Islam is still relatively new to America, there has not been much time to develop Islamic studies curricula in English. 'Iqra International Education Foundation, headed by Dr. Abidullah Ghazi and Tasneema Ghazi, has been a dedicated trailblazer in this area, focusing on texts and materials for weekend "Sunday" schools. Others, such as the Tarbiyah Project with Dawud Tauhidi, are creating and developing entirely new curricula and accompanying materials designed specifically to meet the needs of Muslim children in full time Islamic schools. However, this task is a daunting one because, contrary to the implication in the *Washington Post* article, Islamic schools have no national curriculum and no consensus on whether such a curriculum is even desirable.

Three Areas of Concentration

Once the typical Islamic school has turned the corner on basic survival issues, it begins to develop the resources to tackle the more difficult curriculum decisions. These usually begin with getting rid of the free and used texts and replacing them with texts that reflect the beliefs and values of that school's community. In our pluralistic American society, children need to learn core Islamic values that reflect the teachings of Islam rather than the culture of their parents. To create an educational system that meets these complex needs, one must focus on three areas of concern: pedagogy (art/method of teaching), content (what is taught), and paradigm (a pattern).

Thanks to the tremendous research that has been done on the

brain and learning, educators know quite a bit about how children learn. Knowing how children learn deeply affects pedagogy—the art or method of teaching. The interesting aspect of this is that if we had paid closer attention to the sunnah of our Prophet, we would have discovered it already. Brain-based learning research has documented a concept that we have seen modeled for us by our Prophet, and that is the need to provide a safe and loving environment in which children may learn. The Prophet was known by all to be a loving father, grandfather, and teacher of children. He always spoke kindly to children and allowed them to behave according to their age, adjusting expectations as they grew older and more mature. Intimidation played no part in his role as a teacher. . . .

Modern research has offered an explanation for that which we can infer from our sunnah—when children are afraid, they cannot learn well. The brain will not attend to both fears and facts simultaneously. When a child feels fear, the brain focuses on that fear and dulls attention to other issues. The brain deliberately makes it difficult for children to learn when they are afraid because it is diverting all its energy towards defense strategies and "flight or fight" responses in the body. The simple consequence of this knowledge for educators is to do all we can to decrease fear. When teachers provide a safe and happy environment in which children can learn, they free up more of the children's brainpower to focus on learning.

The second concern of developing a new curriculum is content. We have to decide what our children will learn. In the past, we have relied on overseas and traditional Islamic studies curricula. For a variety of reasons previously discussed, we no longer need or desire to do that. Muslim children born and raised in America face certain challenges that overseas Muslim children do not, and vice versa. The needs of the American-Muslim children must guide us in selecting the concepts, skills, and knowledge that will be our curriculum while rejecting or diminishing others that do not meet these needs. This selecting and rejecting is not an arbitrary process, it is a necessary process. Islam is simply too vast a body of knowledge for anyone to learn it all. Since we cannot learn it all, we must pick and choose what we can learn. Given that core Islamic values are the primary criteria for choosing, the secondary criteria will be the needs of children in a specific culture or situation. For example, American life exposes Muslim teenagers to a rich variety of beliefs and behaviors. Since teens naturally desire to copy their peers, and since most Americans are not Muslim, there is great pressure for Muslim teenagers to conform to behaviors and beliefs that may or may not be in keeping with Islamic teachings. This occurs at a time in their development when they are not fully able to accurately judge differences or withstand pressure to conform. In America, we cannot expect the larger society to push our teenagers closer to Islam. Therefore, teenagers in America are expected to develop a sense of self or identity that is strong enough to withstand the pressures of American society. The curriculum that will develop this strong Islamic identity must first recognize the need for special emphasis on this trait.

On the other hand, teenagers in Saudi Arabia, for example, must develop a sense of their Islamic identity, but not anywhere near what their Muslim-American counterparts need. Saudi Arabia is a very homogeneous society, and its dominant culture is Islam. There is very little need for a Saudi child to develop the internal strength to be different from all his/her classmates or to evaluate the rightness or wrongness of those differences. Saudi children do not need to learn to resist the basic message of the larger society or that of their peers. Became the need for a strong Islamic identity to withstand social pressures is less, the amount of time and importance the Saudi curriculum must place on developing that Islamic identity is reduced.

Consequently, the needs of the two groups of children are different. The primary criterion—developing a strong Islamic identity—guides us to teach this to all children. The secondary criterion—the need to evaluate, select from, and sometimes resist the non-Muslim dominant culture and maintain one's identity as a Muslim—guides us to teach Muslim-American children about self as a much deeper and essential concept. Failure to recognize the difference in needs results in a failure to provide Muslim-American teens with the curricular-based spiritual support and education they need to develop an Islamic identity sufficiently strong to exist in our diverse American society. American life is filled with diversity, and that is very positive. However, children must be given the tools to navigate that diversity. Not all differences are equally valuable; some might even be un-embraceable. Learning to value differences and learning to evaluate differences are essential skills for Muslim children in America.

The Need for a New Paradigm

The third critical component in creating a curriculum for Muslim-American children in Islamic schools is creating a new paradigm, or pattern, of the systematic way information/learning is conceptualized. This new paradigm is the full integration of Islamic teachings and values throughout the entire curriculum.

The traditional educational paradigm assumes instruction through segments. Math class is strictly math and does not concern itself with Islamic values or perspective. Numbers are simply numbers and are to be manipulated and learned. However, in the new paradigm, math becomes more than just numbers, as students learn to explore math with the expectation that Islamic values related to math should be discussed alongside formulas and concepts. Teaching statistics and probabilities in the new paradigm now might involve discussing gambling. How many times can I roll a "7"? When students learn the truth about such probabilities and then connect that to the potential loss of their homes, cars, and even families, that becomes a very powerful integrated math and Islamic studies lesson. The study of math becomes more meaningful to the student's real life, and the Islamic message about the evils of gambling suddenly is more tangible. The new paradigm of infusing Islamic values and perspective throughout a subject-integrated curriculum is foundational to the child learning that Islam is part of every aspect of our lives. Separating Islamic studies from math, science, social studies, etc., sends a powerful subliminal message to students that Islam is irrelevant in "real" life—limited to certain times, places, and circumstances. . . .

From the Fire, Positive Change

The tragic and catastrophic events of 9-11 that created a firestorm of change in the Muslim-American community are having a painful but clearly positive effect on Islamic schools across America. The tragedy created a rapid burning away of the underbrush that so often hindered change, leaving behind a soil laden with rich nutrients ready to nourish the seeds of change. The subsequent emergence of a better-defined Muslim-American identity is helping to clarify the curricular choices that need to be made. The searing heat that was turned on our community has given birth to more than just pain and depression. The seeds of an Islamic renaissance are sprouting in every part of life—educational, professional, political, and spiritual.

As Muslims under fire, we have been forced to examine our personal commitment to Islam. Our identity as Muslims has exploded to the forefront of our public aspect of "self." There is suddenly a horrific cost connected to our choice to be Muslim. Because that cost is so dear, we are no longer willing to accept it merely as an inheritance of our immigrant or convert parents. If this religion could cost us our self-esteem, profession, or even life, we will surely evaluate it deeply. This evaluation is bringing clarity and strength to Muslim-Americans and subsequently to our Islamic schools. Like the knobcone pine, we will arise from this firestorm having benefited from the clarity and seeds of growth left behind.

CHAPTER 5

PERSONAL ACCOUNTS
OF MUSLIMS IN
AMERICA

Contemporary Issues
Companion

THE BACKLASH AFTER THE SEPTEMBER 11 ATTACKS

Mark Singer

The Detroit-area suburb of Dearborn, Michigan, is home to America's largest Arab community. The Muslim population is highly visible and sizable enough to impact the local economy, education, and politics. During periods of discrimination and suspicion, the Muslim community in Dearborn feels particularly vulnerable, as Mark Singer reports in the following article. At no time was this truer than in the first few weeks after the September 11, 2001, terrorist attacks, when this article was written. Singer details the effects of the attacks on Muslims in Dearborn as they deal with bomb scares, racist remarks, and job loss. He focuses on the experiences of several individuals to highlight the concerns of the larger Muslim American populace of Dearborn. Singer is a staff writer for the *New Yorker* literary newsmagazine.

In the summer of 1988, a young Arab-Israeli woman named Maha Mahajneh visited the United States at the invitation of an organization of Palestinian-American women who were holding a convention in New Jersey. It was Mahajneh's first trip to America. At the convention, she gave a talk whose topic was, indirectly, the story of her life: the challenges confronted by Arab citizens of Israel. Mahajneh happened to be an anomalous specimen of upward mobility. Growing up in Umm al-Fahm, a small city in the Galilee, she had longed for three things, at least two of which were out of the question: "I wished I was Jewish, I wished I was a man, and I wished I was rich." Clearly, however, she possessed ample self-confidence and self-awareness. Her family was Sunni Muslim, but far from devout. At eighteen, she left home. By twenty-four, she had a university degree, had settled into a cosmopolitan life in Tel Aviv, and had become the first Palestinian woman certified public accountant in Israel.

Mahajneh went on to deliver the same lecture in Chicago and Detroit, where one member of the audience was Roy Freij, a businessman whose Arabic given name is Raed. At the time of the Six-Day War, in 1967, he had been three years old and living in Jerusalem. In its

Mark Singer, "Home Is Here," *New Yorker*, vol. 77, October 15, 2001, pp. 62–64, 66, 68–70. Copyright © 2001 by Mark Singer. All rights reserved. Reproduced by permission.

aftermath, his parents decided to follow a well-travelled path to south-eastern Michigan, where two hundred and fifty thousand Arabs now reside—other than Paris, the largest concentration outside the Middle East. Months of letter-writing followed Maha and Roy's first encounter, and in the spring of 1989 he flew to Israel and asked her to marry him. Within three weeks, they had wed and Maha had obtained a visa. "I wasn't thinking to come to America at all," she told me. "I came for a man I loved." In 1992, she became a United States citizen.

Maha is the chief financial officer of ACCESS, an Arab social-service and advocacy organization that operates out of eight locations in Dearborn, Michigan, offering, among other things, medical care, psychological counselling, job training and placement, adult education, and after-school programs. Dearborn has a population of a hundred thousand, more than a quarter of which is Arab; in the public schools, the figure is about fifty-eight per cent. For its clients—Lebanese, Syrians, Iraqis, Palestinians, Yemenis, Jordanians, Egyptians, and North Africans—ACCESS, with a comparatively modest annual budget of ten million dollars, is a more vital presence in the community than the Ford Motor Company. Maha's office is in ACCESS's main facility, a converted school building in Dearborn's south end, a dingy district along the perimeter of Ford's gargantuan River Rouge plant.

Threats and Fears

On the morning of September 11th, she awoke at six o'clock and took a two-mile walk in Livonia, the affluent suburb west of Detroit where she lives with her husband and their two young sons. She had dropped the boys at school and was driving to the office while listening to National Public Radio when she heard the first news bulletin about the World Trade Center. Soon after she reached her desk, Maha knew that, while no work would get done that day, she and her colleagues, for symbolic and practical reasons, had to keep the doors open at all of ACCESS's facilities. Except for a three-hour bomb-scare evacuation of one building and a four-day suspension of the after-school program, they succeeded.

The names of Maha and other ACCESS executives are listed on the organization's Web site, and two days after the attack she received an E-mail from a man who attached an inflammatory newspaper column, written by Nolan Finley, an editor at the Detroit *News*, which had appeared in that morning's paper. The "least [Arab and Muslim Americans] can do for their neighbors," Finley insisted, would be to "help in every way possible to smash the network within their own communities that provides money and shelter to terrorists." In other words, what the United States government's intelligence-gathering and law-enforcement apparatus had failed to accomplish before September 11th (or since), the law-abiding Arab citizens of Detroit, in a vigilante spirit that would validate their patriotism, should undertake themselves. The E-mail sender appended his own opinion: "Talk is cheap! If you really love America, turn over the terrorist sympathizers in your midst."

Intemperately, Maha responded in kind: "Your thinking is cheap. It seems to me that you have an IQ of 10???"

In his next message, her pen pal took off the gloves: "Your remark makes it clear you support the vermin that murdered thousands of innocent Americans in New York. . . . I will forward your response to the Detroit *News* and the local FBI. Terrorist scum like you have no right to be in our country."

"I'm the one who's going to forward your stupid remarks to the FBI," Maha replied. "As far as the *News*, I will not be surprised if they have more space for racist remarks from people like you. The way they did from racists like Nolan Finley."

When I paid her a visit, a week later, she seemed burdened by deepening preoccupations.

"The main thing I'm thinking now," she said, "is, after September 11th, how is it going to be for my kids? They were born in this country, and they are totally like other kids. I want my kids to be the President of the United States. Or one will be President. The other will be the adviser. I really want to believe that. At home, the day of the attack, my husband and I sat down with our sons and told them that a bad thing happened and that there might be Arabic people who caused this. We said, 'If someone at school bothers you, you answer back that these people are not representative of the Arab community. You say, "We are Americans, so don't be small-minded and include us in this."' And I keep thinking about the possible retaliation our government might take and the consequences. All our work and accomplishments—are they shattered by what happened in New York? Because we look a certain way? We are not even allowed to grieve like everyone else. People look at us like we are the enemy. I want to say, 'No, I didn't do it. I was on my way to work.' It's like Palestinians living in Israel. They're always under suspicion. And I feel that our situation here might become the same way. And if that happens where do we go? There is no place."

As narratives of immigrant journeys go, Maha's, because it is a love story, seems paradigmatic, even though it is driven neither by economic nor by political urgency. The willingness to uproot oneself and come to America and partake of what is has to offer expresses—more than any appetite for material comfort—a passion for possibility. There has always been a dark side to this evergreen tale, a shadow of dread, a xenophobia rooted not so much in fear of assault from outside aggressors as in a dull-witted suspicion of those among us who look or sound or somehow seem as if they "don't come from around here." Now that the United States actually has been assaulted from the outside, the license to feel suspicious of certain of one's neighbors has been sanctioned as an unfortunate price that the country, at war with an indiscernible foreign enemy, is willing to pay.

A Tense Election Campaign

The migration of Arabs to Detroit in measurable numbers began in the early twentieth century. The first wave of immigrants were mostly Christians from Syria and what is now Lebanon. Muslims, attracted by job opportunities in the automobile industry, started appearing not long thereafter, and since the nineteen-sixties they have predomi-nated, arriving in ripples that emanate from cataclysms in the Middle East—an influx of Palestinians after 1967, followed by Lebanese refugees during the late seventies and early eighties, and Iraqi Shiites in the early nineties. Nothing about the local scenery reminded the earliest arrivals of home, but today certain run-down pockets of southeast Dearborn look as if they might have been grafted on from the West Bank, and in the middle-class neighborhoods there are long commercial stretches with store signs in both Arabic and English. An average of five thousand new Arab immigrants make Detroit their port of entry each year.

In Dearborn, as in New York City, September 11th was a mayoral primary-election day. Unlike New York, Dearborn kept its polls open. The incumbent, Michael Guido, was seeking a fifth term, and al-though he received sixty per cent of the vote, the rules mandate a November runoff against the second-place finisher, Abed Hammoud, a thirty-five-year-old assistant prosecutor, who got eighteen per cent. Hammoud, who is Lebanese, immigrated to the United States in 1990, and likes to say that he landed in America "three days after Saddam moved into Kuwait." This dash of rhetorical color won't hurt with the Iraqi refugee vote, but he would pick that up anyway. Not that it will be enough. No one, with the possible exception of Hammoud him-self, expects him to win.

For a small-city mayor, Guido, a stocky fellow in his mid-forties who favors pin-striped suits, suspenders, and monogrammed shirts with French cuffs, has been quite adept at cultivating an old-school big-city mayoral persona. During his first campaign, in 1985, he circu-lated a blunt-talking pamphlet that referred to Dearborn's "Arab Prob-lem," in which he disparaged bilingual classes for Arab children in the public schools, "new neighbors [who] neglect their property," and the "'gimme, gimme, gimme' attitude" of "the so-called leadership" of the Arab community. Some Dearborn Arabs with long memories place Guido on a continuum that extends back to the heyday of Orville Hubbard, an unapologetic segregationist who was mayor from 1942 to 1977. (Hubbard is most often remembered for promoting the unsubtle motto "Keep Dearborn Clean" and for his role during the 1967 race riots in Detroit, when he took to the street to prohibit blacks from crossing into his city.) Guido has sufficient finesse to have befriended many members of the older Lebanese business establishment. But no one would accuse him of being overly solicitous toward the larger Arab population, and they are grossly underrepresented in the municipal workforce—about two and a half per cent.

Dearborn is arguably the most likely city in America where a mayoral candidate, after outlining his position on street-light maintenance, might be tossed questions about national security and would be expected to answer. Guido knows that most voters aren't all that concerned with local politics at the moment and that the less he says the better. The terrorist attack, he said, "clouds what you can do to separate yourself from your opponent." He continued, "You don't point out that your opponent is Arab-American. You talk about what you can do. What I've done for my city, I blow this guy out of the water—that should be the contest. But, you know, I have people saying, 'I'm voting for you because I don't want to vote for an Arab.' Three people have told me that in the last week. Three people telling you that out loud is like getting ten letters. And the politician's rule of thumb is that ten letters means a thousand people are thinking about it."

Or, as Hammoud said to me the week after the attack, "You think I can go knock on doors now? It's not a good time to campaign."

Seeking Respect

In the spring of 1991, after participating in uprisings against the government of Saddam Hussein, Abu Muslim al-Hayder, a Shiite college professor of computer-control engineering who was then in his mid-thirties, fled Iraq with his wife and four children. They had not been long inside a Saudi Arabian refugee camp when it became evident that it was hardly a refuge. The camp population was infested with spies for the Saddam regime and "the Saudis don't look at us as full human beings—they look at us as prisoners." After the family spent a year and a half in detention, a relief agency called the Church World Service resettled them in Washington State. There al-Hayder went back to school and subsequently tried and failed to find a job in the computer industry. Confident that his bilingual abilities made him employable, in 1995 he moved the family to Detroit.

On September 11th, al-Hayder, who has been a citizen [since 1996], happened to be one of the federal observers dispatched to monitor the municipal election in the town of Hamtramck, ten miles northeast of Dearborn, where there had been discrimination against Arab voters in the past. He was supposed to spend that night in a hotel and file a report the next morning, but he was allowed to leave at 9 P.M. and return to his wife and (now six) children, in Detroit.

"I found all my family scared, afraid that somebody would attack the house," he told me. Most of his neighbors had American flags displayed on their porches, and when he went to a flag store the next day it was sold out. As a short-term approach to making his allegiance plain, he tied an American-flag balloon to his balcony.

Before September 11th, al-Hayder said, he felt happy and secure. He was delighted with his children's progress in school and, in his work as ACCESS's professional liaison to the Iraqi community, he was gratified by the chance to help his newly arrived countrymen. He counts himself far more fortunate than many other erstwhile Iraqi professionals—the college teacher who now delivers pizzas; the widely published literary critic who, having failed at carpentry, is now on welfare. But he is also greatly disturbed by the American media's depiction of Muslims, most of all because of how it might affect his children's perception of themselves.

Al-Hayder has a long familiarity with, and an exceptional equanimity in the face of, the consequences of dissent. In 1978, he was imprisoned by Saddam's predecessor, Ahmad Hassan al-Bakr, and sentenced to death for his political associations, then released a year and a half later when Saddam came to power and issued an amnesty for most political prisoners. Al-Hayder remembers regarding the gesture with skepticism. "I didn't trust Saddam," he said, "because I knew that even if he gives you something he will take a lot of things more valuable."

If he saved your life, I asked, how could he take from you something more valuable?

"There are many things more valuable than your life. There is your dignity, your respect. If you live a life with no respect, it's better to die. And this is why I agreed to come to America as a refugee—better than to stay in Saudi Arabia or go to another country. But this crisis we are in is making many people, especially the media, turn away from the values that I know. If someone comes and tries to insult me for no reason, I cannot tell him thank you. A lot of people now who are colored and are American citizens, and who have a right to have weapons, may go and get a license to have weapons to defend themselves. I may even lose faith in law-enforcement agencies because they target people who are Arab and Muslims. And this is very disturbing. None of this is why I came here. I came here to be a respected human being.". . .

Discrimination and Uncertainty

Ahmed Mohamed Esa is a short, slightly built, soft-voiced forty-eight-year-old man with a cropped white beard, black hair, a gap between his front teeth, and thick dark rings beneath his eyes. Since 1976, he has divided his life between Yemen and Dearborn, where he shares with two other Yemenis a five-hundred-dollar-a-month three-room flat. In Yemen, Esa has a wife and six sons. They live three hours from the city of Taiz, in Makbana, a village with no telephone and no electricity. None of them have ever seen America. Until the day after the attack on the World Trade Center, Esa had worked at a small welding company for fifteen years—longer than everyone except the company's owner, Paul Rakoczy. He earned $12.36 an hour and usually put in an eight-and-a-half-hour day. Whatever money he saved he sent to his wife, unless he was bringing it in person; each year, he spends at least three or four months with his family.

On September 12th [2001], Esa told me, he arrived at the welding shop at 5:40 A.M.—around the time the muezzin at his neighborhood mosque was uttering the morning prayer call—and punched the clock. Then: "I go take my work uniform. When I hear the whistle for the work, I take my coffee and go to take my gloves and go to see Mr. Paul what I work on today. He say complete the job from yesterday I start to work. I'm working twenty minutes, a half hour, and he say to me, 'Don't work. Go home.' I tell him, 'Why I go home?' He say, 'You are Arabic, you are Muslim. You don't see what happened in New York, in Washington? You don't see how many people your people killed?' I tell him I not do nothing. I work here. I have been here fifteen years. How I can go home? He say, 'I can see your face. Go pray in your mosque. Go pray with your leader. I don't want you to work here.' For a half minute or a minute, I thinking what I can do. He say, 'If you don't go, I get the police for you.' I hear that, I say maybe there is trouble, so I go. I have my check coming the next day, but I don't go get it. I'm too scared. I think maybe if I go there he do something, I don't know."

After finding his way to an ACCESS counselling center, Esa told his story to me and to a reporter for the *Free Press*, who in turn tracked down Rakoczy. Though Rakoczy disputed elements of Esa's account—he had not fired him outright but had told him to take the rest of the week off—he made no attempt to conceal his feelings about Islam. "As far as I'm concerned, their religion is done," he said. "When these guys ran their plane in there like that and hurt all those people, that was the end of it right there. That made their religion—you might as well write it as I say it—the scum of the earth." (In October 2001, a lawyer for Esa filed a discrimination suit against Rakoczy.)

I asked Esa whether his wife knew that the family no longer had an income.

"I speak to her sometimes once a week, sometimes once a month," he said. "If she come to the city, she will call. She doesn't know what happened with my job. She maybe doesn't know what happened in New York. I maybe will talk to her today. Maybe tomorrow."

When I asked whether he had plans to look for another job, he smiled, shrugged, and said, "How can I face an American guy and ask him to work? How can I knock the door and say I'm an Arabic guy? He might kill me."

So what was he planning to do next?

He smiled and shrugged again.

"America has changed like the weather. You not see America how is it? I sleep on Monday. I get up in the morning on Tuesday. Now I don't know what tomorrow will happen. Tomorrow. I don't know. Tomorrow is too far."

MY ISLAMIC ROOTS, MY AMERICAN HOME

Tarannum Kamlani

Muslim journalist Tarannum Kamlani was living in New York City at the time of the September 11, 2001, terrorist attacks. In the following piece, Kamlani relates how her life changed after the tragedy occurred. She explains that her American friends inundated her with questions about Islam and the mind-set of Muslims in the Middle East. However, Kamlani writes, although she was raised Muslim, her upbringing was primarily secular and Western, and she was uncomfortable with suddenly being considered an expert on Islam. The author describes how she sought out a Muslim community in New York in order to gain a better understanding of Islam. At the same time, Kamlani confides, she was confronted with the painful realization that many non-Muslim Americans thought of her as an outsider. Kamlani currently lives and works in Toronto, Canada.

As I sat at my computer in my Brooklyn apartment that morning of Sept. 11, 2001, a message flashed onto my screen from a friend in Denmark—telling me to turn on my television. Not that it was necessary, because all I had to do was look out my window, across the East River to Manhattan. My clear view of those slim grey-blue towers beyond Brooklyn's stubby brownstone houses had been transformed into a scene from a really bad Hollywood action movie. I watched the World Trade Center's twin towers on fire, and then saw them collapse as though made of talcum powder.

Explaining Islam

Up to that morning, Islam had played a significant but fairly quiet role in my life. I was born in India and raised a Muslim in a tiny Persian Gulf country, the United Arab Emirates (UAE). A British accent was starched and ironed into my voice by British schools there, and later at university in England. [In summer 2001] fresh out of journalism school, I was very unemployed. Until Sept. 11, I had come across, I think, as an interesting and odd foreign person to most Americans I

Tarannum Kamlani, "My Islamic Roots, My American Home," *Maclean's*, September 16, 2002, p. 56. Copyright © 2002 by Maclean Hunter Canadian Publishing, Ltd. Reproduced by permission of the author.

met. When the identities and histories of the hijackers became known—Mohammed Atta, for instance, had a UAE passport—that began to change. People I knew began asking me to "explain" Islam; their questions ranged from hysterical—"why are they doing this to us?"—to the usual well-meaning inquiries about why Islam oppressed women.

Despite some discomfort at suddenly being regarded as an authority on such things, I was in many ways grateful, because, at the same time, the television networks were airing seemingly endless scenes of people in the Middle East, Pakistan and Afghanistan, of veiled women and angry bearded men, saying that America had gotten what it deserved. I spent hours trying to remind myself that this was far removed from the Islam I grew up with—and explaining to people that my middle-class, suburban, mostly secular upbringing bore no resemblance to what they saw on TV.

As Americans woke up to this part of the world that had presented itself in such frightening form, I, and others like me—South Asian, Arab, Muslim—had to deal with a part of ourselves that we could not deny: one that set us apart as people to be wary of in the minds of some, and regarded as outright enemies in America's war on terror by others. This new scrutiny and alarm about Islam forced me to try to better understand it, both as a person and as a journalist.

Reaching Out

With stories of hate crimes against South Asians and Muslims mounting in the days immediately after the attacks, I went off in search of a Muslim community in New York. I wanted to communicate their fears and outrage at what had happened to the rest of the world in my capacity as a journalist. It meant having to reach out to people in a religious setting in which I do not often find myself—Friday afternoon prayers at a mosque, traditionally a time when the community gets together.

So on Sept. 14, the first Friday after the attacks, I presented myself at a small mosque in the East Village in Manhattan, not far from Ground Zero. It had been established by Bangladeshi immigrants in the 1970s. This community had lost many of its members when the towers fell. The mosque had been subject to some related backlash. But as the trustees told me, they had also received tremendous support from non-Muslim neighbours, some of whom chased away demonstrators calling for the mosque to be destroyed or removed. I came away heartened at being able to write a positive story and grateful for the unexpected comfort I found in the prayer service.

One of "Them"

But I was constantly confronted by the feeling of being one of "them," and not knowing quite what to do about it. A few months later, I found myself working at the *New York Times*, putting together collected mini-obituaries and profiles of the people lost on Sept. 11 for a book version of the newspaper's series "Portraits of Grief." This involved regular contact with victims' families and friends. Every so often, a grieving spouse or parent would say, "That's an unusual name you have," or a flirtatious firefighter would ask, "So where did you get that accent?"—immediately followed by "Where are you from?" I was never more glad than to be able to answer "India." I would say this while silently offering a prayer in praise of my grandparents, who opted to stay in India [instead of moving to Pakistan] at the time of partition in 1947. It was a strange and unwelcome feeling, but I couldn't bear the thought of being thought of by this group, of all people, as one of "them."

The last year has forced everyone to reassess something in our lives, be it relationships with estranged family members, acceptable levels of patriotic fervour, or depths of religious devotion. For me, and others like me, born and raised in a part of the world that terrifies the one that we now live in, it has meant trying harder than ever not to get caught in the purported "Clash of Civilizations"—and using our knowledge and understanding of both to somehow try to make some sense of it all.

A Schoolgirl in the Nation of Islam

Sonsyrea Tate

The Nation of Islam originated in the United States in the 1930s, attracting impoverished African Americans through its message of black empowerment and hope. Sonsyrea Tate's grandparents joined the Nation of Islam in the 1950s, and she was raised as a third-generation Black Muslim during the 1970s, an experience she recounts in her book *Little X: Growing Up in the Nation of Islam.* The following excerpt begins in 1976, after the University of Islam, the private Muslim school that Tate attended, was closed due to lack of funds. Tate describes her mixed emotions about transferring to a public elementary school, her attempts to fit in with her non-Muslim classmates, and her feelings of isolation. A freelance journalist, Tate serves on the faculty of the World Journalism Institute in Asheville, North Carolina.

It was April 1976 when our Muslim school closed down and I had to transfer to a public school, two months before their school year ended. It was chilly outside the morning Ma walked us to Kingsman Elementary to enroll us. Inside, the walls along the empty corridors were painted a sickly greenish blue color, and the odor wafting from the cafeteria smelled nothing like the wholesome beef burgers and wheat doughnuts I used to buy after school at the Temple.

I missed Sister Memphis who used to greet us at the door with a welcoming "As-Salaam-Alaikum" every morning. And I missed Vernarda, Kim, Saundra, Nynita, Aisha, and the other young Muslim sisters with whom I had shared friendships and a very comfortable sense of sameness. They had transferred to the schools in their own neighborhoods. At my new school, my languid, long clothes distinguished me from my classmates, who were wearing fashionably tight designer jeans. I was moving into new territory and wasn't sure what to expect.

A Lot to Learn

Growing up in the Nation of Islam and then having to go out into the real world was like moving to another country, adjusting to a culture and philosophy we had been trained to despise. As enthusiastic as I was about seeing how the other people lived, I also was nervous about how I would fit in. I wondered if they would like me and welcome me like a sister since they were black like me or if I would find out that they really were mean and uncivilized, as I had been taught. Maybe they would teach me their games, which I hadn't had a chance to learn in the Nation, and maybe I could teach them some facts about how great we black people really are, which they didn't learn out in the world.

I was wearing a long orange and brown patchwork dress with a white headpiece for my first day of school. [My brother] Darren looked like a normal kid in regular pants and a pullover shirt.

Darren, for the most part, was simply overjoyed because he knew that the teachers in public schools couldn't put their hands on him or even make him stand in a corner with his hands folded across the top of his head like they used to do at the Muslim school. Darren's close-cut haircut was the only thing that distinguished him from the other boys, who wore short Afros.

As a Muslim boy Darren enjoyed a certain level of respect in our neighborhood. As a Muslim girl, I was respected, too, but it was a different kind of respect. It would keep boys from catcalling out to me, but it would not thwart the taunts of girls who thought Muslim women were crazy or weak for allowing men to dictate what we wore and how we behaved.

We had a lot to learn about people out in the world, and they had a lot to learn about us, too.

The First Day of School

On the first day of school, Ma marched us up to the principal's office. Dressed in pants, a long top down to her knees, and a matching scarf on her head, Ma looked like the myth of the meek Muslim woman. The secretaries turned to watch as we blew into the office. Within moments the myth would be destroyed.

The school principal, Mr. Moore, greeted Ma from behind the linoleum-topped counter and shoved several papers across the divide for Ma to sign. Ma snatched them up and held them close. She knew to read things thoroughly and ask a few questions before signing. Seemed like she was always at odds with official types. Now she was arguing with Mr. Moore because he wanted to put me in the fourth grade with other kids my age while Ma insisted I finish out the sixth grade, since that's what grade I was in at the Muslim school.

Ma wasn't mean or nasty, just serious and unyielding. She didn't smile a lot or turn on any feminine charm to get Mr. Moore to see her point. I was so glad my mother wasn't a weak pushover or a tight-clothes-wearing floozy like some of the other mothers I noticed around our neighborhood.

"No," Ma told Mr. Moore frankly, she would not take us back to the neighborhood clinic for polio, measles, and chicken pox shots.

"I have decided against immunizing my children," she told him.

"I'm sorry, Mrs. Tate. It is the policy of our school system to require complete immunization of all our students," Mr. Moore intoned.

"I understand your policy, sir. But as a parent, I have the right to decide whether or not to immunize my children," she said. "My children have had the chicken pox already, and if and when God sees fit for them to come down with something else, I'll keep them home and take care of them."

Finally, Mr. Moore pointed to the space where she could offer her explanation. "I conscientiously object" was all she wrote. But I knew the real reason was because she didn't trust any agency of the U.S. government to inject anything into the arms of her children. She had explained to us earlier that experimental medicines are tested at the free clinics in black neighborhoods. She had learned this, she said, when she used to work as a nurse at D.C. General Hospital.

Shortly before the lunch bell rang, Mr. Moore guided us up two flights of stairs, where we dropped Darren off at his classroom. Ma told Darren's teacher that she and Dad would support his disciplinary actions against Darren with a strong arm at home. Darren sucked his teeth and sighed. How could she set him up like that?

When we walked through the door of my new classroom, all the kids stopped what they were doing to stare at the small girl in the long orange and brown patchwork dress and white turban on her head. I looked past them and noticed the bulletin board with the "A" papers from last week's vocabulary test. Immediately, I determined I was smarter. *Atmosphere*, I thought to myself, we learned that word in the fourth grade. Above the blackboards, which were actually green, there were small placards with science and history information. This science and history would also be a breeze compared to what we had studied at the University of Islam.

My new teacher, Mrs. Hardin, was a round and robust woman, her skin the color of oak wood. She rose from her desk where she had been picking out the bones from her fish sandwich when we walked in.

"Good morning," she said, smiling is she walked over to us. "You must be Mrs. Tate."

"Yes." Ma smiled back, extending her hand for a shake. "And this is Sons-Sere-Ray," pronouncing it phonetically.

"Class, say good morning to Sons-Sere-Ray," Mrs. Hardin commanded.

"What kind of name is that?" one of my classmates demanded from the front row.

"It's Indian. It means 'Morning Star,'" I said with pride.

"Is that some kind of Moozlem name?" he persisted.

"It's Indian," I repeated more forcefully.

This was a few years before African American parents began naming their children foreign names and names the parents themselves created. Before inner-city mothers across the country would look at their daughters and name them Imani because they wanted them to know they represented "Faith." Before a father named Shawn and a mother named Nina would put their heads together and come up with the name "Shawnina."

To Pledge Allegiance?

At school the next morning, when I declined to rise with the rest of the class for the Pledge of Allegiance, followed by a run-through of "America the Beautiful," Terry Gomillion, a dark-skinned, bubbly girl who sat to the right of me, wanted to know why.

"Because the United States doesn't care about black people," I told her.

"What do you mean? It's just a little thing we say and a little song," she said.

"It's not just a little song," I said with the earnestness of someone trying to enlighten a poor fool.

Elijah Muhammad had trained us well. At the University of Islam, the only flag to which we pledged our allegiance was the flag representing the Nation of Islam, and the song we sang at the beginning of our Monday morning assemblies was the Muslim fight song.

In fact, we had learned to despise the American flag. The red in the American flag, we were taught, represented the blood of the slaves, our forefathers. The white represented the skin color of our oppressors. And the blue represented the illusion that white people continually created for blacks. "When you look at the sky, it appears blue," the minister used to teach on Sunday. "But it is not really blue. Blue is the color of illusion. When you look at the water, it appears blue. But it is not." And the fifty stars in the American flag represented how divided was the country. The Muslim flag had one star, representing one Nation, unified.

Now how would I explain all of this to my eleven-year-old classmate, who clearly was not as enlightened as I?

"It's not just a little song," I said. "Every time you sing it, you're supporting the government. The government brought black people over here as slaves and still, even today, refuses to treat black people fairly," I said.

Difficulties at Recess

Mrs. Hardin interrupted our chatter and told us to do our work. We completed a few verb-subject agreement assignments, then were told to read a section in our history book. By the time the bell rang for recess, the girls' curiosity had temporarily vanished. It was play time. Out on the blacktop playground, Terry invited me to jump double dutch, a game I had not yet learned.

"Sonsyrea, all you gotta do is this," Terry said, half bouncing on the balls of her feet, about to jump into the twirling ropes. "All, all, all, all . . ." the girls sang a tune for her to jump to. After several minutes of fancy spins and high jumps in the ropes, Terry exited the ropes to give me a chance. She saw that I didn't knew how to jump. "Come on. Hold your dress like this," she said, drawing my long dress up to my knees. "Okay, okay," I said, while the other girls started the tune over for me. "Jump in!" one of the girls shouted as they started the tune over again. I finally jumped in, and instead of finding harmony in the ropes. I found myself tangled among them. The girls all laughed, all except Terry. She could see that I was embarrassed.

"Okay. Just try it again," she said. She was such an upbeat kind of girl. I liked her a lot. I tried it a few more times before the girls' laughter became too much.

"That's why Elijah Muhammad forbade sport and play anyway," I thought to myself. "I never had to worry about jumping double dutch to win approval at the Muslim school. Our grades were the only thing that mattered. Whoever got the most As got the most attention." I wished I was back at the Muslim school, back among friends, among girls who looked and behaved like me. As I stood alone with my thoughts on a playground full of children, Darren ran past me and I called out to him, but he kept running like he didn't hear me. "DARREN!" I called again, but he was out of earshot now. I hated when he tried to pretend like he didn't see me, like by ignoring me somebody might not realize that the girl in the long clothes and turban was his sister. But anybody could tell we were related, we looked just alike.

As the days passed, I began to feel shy and alienated. During the next few weeks, during recess out on the playground, I got tired of my classmates' stupid questions: "Do y'all have hair? I heard Muslim girls were bald headed."

"How come y'all can't eat pork?" someone would ask.

"Because it gives you worms," I'd answer.

"Don't you miss eating ham and pork chops and stuff?" someone else might inquire.

"Nope. Never tasted it."

"Never?"

"Who said it gives you worms? It don't give you no worms. I eat it and I didn't get worms. People don't get worms. . . ."

"People do get worms, they just can't see them. They get little tiny worms inside their stomachs and get sick with all kinds of diseases," I explained.

"Y'all missing some good stuff. You can't eat pickled pigs' feet, either?"

"The pig is the nastiest animal on the face of the Earth. The pig is grafted from the rat, cat, and dog," I said, sounding kind of robotic by now.

When Darren and I would go home for lunch, I was thankful for the respite. There were two more months of this playground dialogue before finally it was graduation day.

A Poem on Graduation Day

On June 12, all the wooden seats in the hot auditorium were filled with the joyful faces of mothers in Sunday dresses and fathers in slacks and button-down shirts. I looked around to find my relatives. Only they would understand why I was the only child there in this stupid long light blue dress and matching headpiece while the other girls wore white dresses.

At first Ma wasn't going to let me participate in the ceremony because she said that the society shouldn't be making us think that we've accomplished something by completing sixth grade. "You'll graduate when you finish high school," she said. But [my grandmother], GrandWillie, finally persuaded Ma—the day before the ceremony—to let me participate.

GrandWillie and I shopped around and could not find a long white dress anywhere. So here I was in a long polyester light blue dress with a panel of spring flowers down the front. I was very angry at Ma for making me such an oddball. I was out in the world now and thought she should let me dress like everybody else. Walking down the aisle with the other little girls in short white dresses and shiny curls in their hair, I felt like an ugly duck. At home, my uncles had always told me how pretty I was, and among others in the Nation the little girls in short dresses would have felt ugly, but I was out in the world now.

I was glad when I spotted GrandWillie's turban in the back of the auditorium. Dad couldn't be there because he had to work, but I didn't mind because he was doing what daddies were supposed to do. Ma was home, too swollen with her latest pregnancy to leave the house. But GrandWillie was there, and so were Grandma and Granddaddy Thomas. I raised my dress a bit when it came time for me to walk onstage to do my poem, so I wouldn't trip. I stood behind the podium, and the audience laughed when they saw that I couldn't reach the microphone even standing on my tiptoes. The audience thought this was cute, but I wasn't there to be cute. I was there to deliver a poem. Someone brought me a step stool and I began:

I have to live with myself and so,
I want to be fit for myself to know.
I want to be able as days go by,
Always to look myself straight in the eye.

I recited it slowly and with as much drama as I could muster. I stood poised and spoke with conviction, just like I had rehearsed it.

I don't want to stand with the setting sun,
And hate myself for the things I've done.

I want to go out with my head erect.
I want to deserve all men's respect.
But here in the struggle for fame and wealth,
I want to be able to like myself.

It was a good thing I had learned to like myself in the Nation of Islam, a good thing I had learned I was smart and decent and good all the way through. Out in the real world, I was beginning to realize that I often would have to stand alone.

After I finished my poem, our school choir stood to sing a song I'd heard them rehearse for weeks:

Oh, freedom, oh, freedom, oh, freedom over me
And before I be a slave, I be buried in my grave
And go home to my lord and be free.

The ceremony was full of poems, songs, and speeches. Our principal congratulated us on having completed the first phase of our education and told us that at the next level, junior high school, we would have more freedoms and therefore would have to be more responsible for ourselves.

My classmates were lucky, I thought. All they had to think about were the changes in school. I had to worry about going to a new school, fitting in out in the world, *and* changes in the religion that had been my way of life.

Changing Paths: Converting to Islam

Carol L. Anway

Carol L. Anway is a Christian writer and educator whose daughter, Jodi, converted to Islam shortly after her marriage to a Muslim man. Struggling to accept her daughter's decision, Anway began to learn more about Islam and spoke to other women who had become Muslim for various reasons. Eventually, Anway sent a questionnaire to American women who had converted to Islam and incorporated her findings in the book *Daughters of Another Path: Experiences of American Women Choosing Islam*. The following selection begins with Anway's description of her personal reaction to the news of Jodi's conversion. The author also relates the experiences of several other women as they started on their own paths toward becoming Muslim.

We were with Jodi for two days one summer attending a friend's wedding. She and Reza had been married for two years and were studying at the University of Arkansas, about an eight-hour drive from our home. She seemed so different, yet I liked her mature manner and her kindness. When making a hair appointment, she was careful to insist on a female rather than a male beautician. Even though it was in the middle of a hot summer, she wore long sleeves. Her conversation was serious as she spoke of what she was learning about Islam.

On the way to the wedding, we talked. Jodi sat with her dad in the front seat. She turned around to look at me sitting in the backseat and said, "Mom, who do you believe Jesus was?"

"Well, Jodi, you know. You've been going to church all your life," I replied.

"But, Mom, I want to hear you tell me now."

And so I told her what I thought was basic to the Christian belief of Jesus' birth, of his ministry, of his being the Son of God, of his death and resurrection for our salvation.

"Then Jesus is God?" Jodi asked.

"Yes, Jesus is part of the Trinity," I replied, "and throughout his teaching and ministry, he points us toward God."

Carol L. Anway, *Daughters of Another Path: Experiences of American Women Choosing Islam*. Lee's Summit, MO: Yawna Publications, 1996. Copyright © 1996 by Carol L. Anway. All rights reserved. Reproduced by permission.

I felt frustrated. Somehow her responses left me feeling inadequate. Why couldn't I do better? Even though she didn't say so, I could feel her moving toward an Islamic viewpoint. *Well, no chance of her going all the way,* I comforted myself.

All too soon Jodi was gone again, back into the world of university studies with her husband, Reza. We, too, returned to our home and jobs. We kept in touch with Jodi by phone. With each call, we felt the gap widening. She was a natural at imitating others and often sounded like an Iranian trying to learn English as she imitated her friends' accents. She talked of cooking—not American foods but Iranian cuisine. She spoke only of her Muslim friends—not Christian or even American friends. We couldn't quite define it, but there was a shift.

November came and Jodi and Reza came home for Thanksgiving. We had been apprehensive but looked forward to it. We really loved those two, and we missed them. Jodi came through the door. She was wearing a long dress over her jeans and sweater. She carried a scarf in her hand, and her hair was flat against her head. We embraced, then sat and talked in a rather stilted, surface manner. It was late and time to retire. Reza went out to carry in the suitcases. As I got up, Jodi came over by me.

"Mom, I need to talk to you."

I turned my back and headed for the kitchen. Tears were welling up in my eyes. No, I wouldn't talk with her. I couldn't stand what I thought she had to say. "Not now," I answered without looking at her.

The next day was Thanksgiving. We were all heading to Grandma's house, an hour's drive away. "Mom, we won't be eating the turkey or dressing. We're only eating approved meats."

Well, big deal! See if I care! I wouldn't look at or acknowledge her. She had the long dress on over her jeans again, and as we walked out the door, she put on the scarf so it covered all her hair. I sat in the front seat and sulked the entire trip. The rest of the family seemed to carry on as usual—Reza and Jodi, her two brothers, and her dad. I managed to avoid her the whole day until that night back at the house.

"Mom, we have to talk."

"I don't want to hear it."

"You've got to hear it, Mom, please." I finally gave in, and we sat down.

"Mom, I've converted to Islam. I was already Muslim this summer, but I wasn't ready to tell you then. I needed to grow stronger before I told you."

Daughters Learning of a New Path

The signs are often there that our young adults are changing from the path we want for them, yet we aren't sure just what to do about it. Consequently, we frequently ignore it, hoping the whole situation will go away, and we won't have to deal with it. As young adults, our children are beyond our control; they encounter many new ideas and new perspectives in the world, and they make their own decisions.

Of the respondents to the questionnaire, 63 percent were married to Muslims before their conversions. Their attitudes toward Islam at the time of marriage ranged from fear of Islam to having already investigated Islam on their own. Twenty-three percent converted before marriage and later met and married a Muslim, while 6 percent who converted are still single. Only one woman responded as having become Muslim even though married to a white, American, non-Muslim male.

None of these women felt compelled by their husbands to study Islam and convert. In many instances it was the searching of the wife that drew the husband back into practice of his religion. These Muslim men (often not practicing) seemed, for the most part, to be well-versed in their religion. It wasn't a case of not knowing what Islam was and what it required; it was being away from family in a land where it was difficult to practice Islam that fostered less involvement. Family responsibilities and a searching, supportive wife naturally drew them again into the practice of their faith.

Although the stories of these women vary in the specifics, there are many commonalities in their introduction and conversion to Islam. The majority of women were introduced to Islam by the husband. Others were introduced by classes they took in college, and a few by acquaintance with Muslim neighbors or from having visited in an Islamic country. Islam touched in them a need they felt. Each in her own way chose to accept Islam and make shahada, declaring herself as Muslim by acknowledging "There is no God but Allah and Muhammad is a messenger of Allah." The following stories help us gain a sense of the variety of ways they learned about Islam and the conversion experiences that brought these women to the point of declaration.

The Witness of the Significant Other

The desire to further a relationship with a Muslim who had become a significant other was a motivator for some to investigate Islamic beliefs more seriously.

> I met my husband in 1983. Prior to that I held all the common stereotypes of Islam, that it was medieval, subjugated women, and was violent. I never had any formal exposure to Islam despite a master's level education. Although not practicing the prayers or fasting regularly, my husband was very sure that Islam was the true religion of God. I was aware that although I was under no obligation to convert, he would not marry me without my committing to raise any children we would have as Muslims. I felt he had a sound value system and my initial exposure to the Qur'an did not convince me

one way or the other, but I saw nothing I felt adverse about in raising our children Muslim.

In 1988, our first son was 18 months old. Our marriage was in deep trouble for a variety of reasons. I turned to the Qur'an to find ways I could use it to manipulate my husband into counseling. Our conflict reached a zenith in September, 1988, and I asked him for a separation. I felt I had no options, even though I still loved him. I was calm driving to work. Out of my soul came an intense pain, and I cried out loud for God to help me. At that moment I recognized my desire to be Muslim, and it did not matter if my marriage broke up or not. I wanted to be Muslim for me.

I met my husband at Louisiana Tech University. He didn't want to have an illegal relationship with me, so he immediately proposed marriage, asked me if I was interested in reading about Islam and becoming Muslim, and he actually asked me to put a cover on my hair.

I was insulted by the last two requests, and at eighteen, I wasn't sure I wanted to get married. I was attracted to him and wanted to be with him. He discontinued contact with me. I went home and read on my own about Islam. I changed and wanted to marry him.

[From one who was unchurched] My husband was supportive in helping me put my life together. I was recovering once again from emotional problems. He really had very little to do with my conversion. He introduced me to Islam but never asked me to convert. Islam does not require me to, but he returned fully to his religion. As I saw him gradually acquire an inner peace, I became envious. Inner peace was what I sought. So I asked for literature. The more I read, the more I wanted to learn. Islam means "submission to the will of God" or "inner peace." I felt God himself was leading me.

The Witness of Muslim Neighbors and Acquaintances

. . . Some of the young women met Muslims in this country who influenced them by their daily living and practice. They sensed in the Muslims personal strength that seemed to come from their beliefs. Sometimes the Muslims' witness was verbal as they responded to questions, but more often it was how they chose to live their lives.

I was fifteen years old when I first started to learn about Islam. A Saudi family moved in next door, and I was fascinated by their behavior, dress, language, and religion. The wife and I became very close, but it took four years for me to convert. They never pushed it on me, they simply answered my questions and showed me great kindness and hospitality. All throughout high school, though I was not a Muslim, I stayed away from negative elements. It came from my Saudi friends' influence. So when I converted, the only real things I changed were my clothing and leisure time activities such as concerts, movies, and sports. . . .

In 1983, through friends I met an Arab woman, and we became best friends. One day she asked if I could babysit her daughters, and I did. One night before the kids went to bed they told me their prayers and also wanted to teach me. The next day, she asked me if I considered Jesus the Son of God. I replied, "Really, I have no religion but tell me more about your religion, Islam." It took me two more years from then to say shahada.

I volunteered to help tutor Saudi women who were studying English as a second language. I found it odd that these women refused to have a man tutor them, but after checking out and reading several books on Islam from the public and school libraries, I began to understand these "mysterious" ladies in black. The women began to open up more and more and invited me into their homes and my knowledge of Islam unfolded. I really respected the religion as I saw it practiced on a daily basis.

It was in the spring of 1988 that I really began to practice. I contacted the local Islamic Association and joined a sister's Qur'an study group. There I met sisters who were and still are great role models and guiding forces for me yet today.

The impact of devout and dedicated Muslims on the lives of these women supports the church growth principle that in Christianity most are converted to a church because of someone they know who influences their lives toward accepting Christ and the church. These women sensed that living as a Muslim fulfilled these people spiritually and they, too, wanted to feel very close to God by being a true Muslim.

Learning About Islam in the College Setting

Many of the women made contact with Islam for the first time in the college setting. It may have been through specific religion courses, books they read for general college classes, or Muslim students or friends they associated with on campus. Hearing about Islam greatly interested them.

I was meeting with a group of international students as part of a conversation group program to practice English. As I listened to a Palestinian man talk about his life, his family, his faith, it struck a nerve in me. The more I learned about Islam the more I became interested in it as a possibility for my own life.

The following term the group disbanded, but I registered for a class "Introduction to Islam." This class brought back all the concerns I had about Christianity. As I learned about Islam, all of my questions were answered. All of us are not punished for Adam's original sin. Adam asked God for forgiveness and our merciful and loving God forgave him. God doesn't require a blood sacrifice in payment for sin. We must sincerely ask for forgiveness and amend our ways. Jesus wasn't God; he was a prophet like all the other prophets. They all taught the same message: believe in the One true God, worship and submit to God alone, and live a righteous life according to the guidance he has sent.

This answered all my questions about the Trinity and the nature of Jesus (all God, all human, or a combination?). God is a perfect and fair judge, who will reward or punish us based on our faith and righteousness. I found a teaching that put everything in its proper perspective, and appealed to my heart and intellect. It seemed natural. It wasn't confusing. I had been searching. I found a place to rest my faith.

I was in college taking psychology and sociology but felt a need to turn back to religion even though I didn't agree with Christianity a whole lot, especially the way it had been presented to me before in life. After shopping around at all the different religions like Hinduism, Buddhism, I enrolled in the religious studies class in college and took literature of the Old Testament. One of the things that came up was going back to look at the roots of Christianity. It seemed that Christianity was okay then, but it got changed to the point to where women were not really accepted, as well as other changes. Reading through the texts, I came across things that the pastors in our church had never talked about. It really shook me, and it made me begin to question the Bible.

My husband gave me a Qur'an as a wedding gift, and it just sat on the shelf during the time I was taking the religion classes. After that we went to Syria to visit the family. I couldn't speak the language so I had a lot of time on my hands. So I read the whole thing, and while reading it I was looking for things that seemed incorrect or were problems to me. I came across things in the English translation that bothered me, like "Lightly beat your wife." So I would say to my husband, "How can you believe this stuff?" Then he would say, "No, in Arabic that's not the way it really is," and would explain from the original. I went through the whole thing and couldn't find anything inaccurate. And I thought, "Well, this is better than anything else I've seen." I converted in 1988.

Searching to Fill the Spiritual Void

. . . Many of the respondents were searching for something in the spiritual area to fill the void in their lives. It was through this openness that many began to receive the pull toward Islam. This need is reflected in most of the descriptions the women give of their conversion experience. They may have come to the conversion point from a variety of situations, but most were receptive because of the need within themselves and the gentle persuasion of the Muslim person or resource which touched their hearts and souls.

> I married someone who was not a Christian and we both were non-practicing in anything religious. I still thought of myself as a Christian. "What else is there," I thought. I still held my belief of God and his creation of the earth, but wasn't sure of the other beliefs I was taught growing up.

> The year after my divorce in 1990 I started thinking about what I needed, about what I believed. Early in 1991 I started checking books out of the library and reading about Islam, more because I was curious about it than anything. I slowly read books on it, but also lived my life as I had been living it. It wasn't until the fall of 1992 that I decided I had to do something about it—either get serious about studying it or forget about it. I found several American Muslim sisters in Manhattan, twenty miles from where I lived in a very small town. I studied with them and learned the practical aspects of what I had read for the past year and a half. I took my shahada in December 1992. . . .

> I was first introduced to Islam at the age of fourteen, but because of family conflicts I was not able to learn or practice. After leaving home to go to college, I had the freedom to pursue the religion. The biggest change I had to make (besides the obvious ones of dress, diet, etc.) was to put some distance between myself and my family and former friends. I did this as a protection for myself that would allow me to grow stronger in my religion without distractions. I had little sense of loss because I filled the void with newfound Muslim friends, and later, my husband.

Many of the women have expressed their growing respect and love for the Qur'an, which is considered the final and literal word of God.

For some women the Qur'an was an important part of their conversion experience.

> My conversion began as the result of a challenge by a Muslim to read the Qur'an in order for us to have a debate on the position of women in Islam. I held the stereotypical view of Muslim women as being oppressed and in a bad position relative to their Christian counterparts. I was nominally Christian, raised in a Catholic environment, but was not practicing the religion and really only bothered to label myself a Christian in order not to appear too rebellious in front of my extended family (my family was also really only Christian in name, not "reality").
>
> The reading of the Qur'an and of hadith of the Prophet is what captured me. I went through a very odd experience whereby for the whole week it took me to read the Qur'an I couldn't sleep and seemed to toss and turn all night in a feverish sweat. I had strange and vivid dreams about religious topics, and when I would get up all I wanted to do was continue reading the Qur'an. I didn't even study for my final exams which were happening at the same time!
>
> I began a course in Middle Eastern History, which immersed me further into the study of Islam. When the professor read passages from the Qur'an to illustrate how powerful a "tool" it was in spreading Islam throughout the world, my heart sang. I knew I had found the TRUTH! I had been searching for God since the early '80s. At this point I knew I would someday be a Muslim. After the class was over I continued my investigation into Islam. I bought an English translation of the Qur'an and read it daily. I was living at home at the time so hid most of this from my family. I got together often with my new friends and my total lifestyle began to change.

. . . This holy book, the Qur'an, so revered by Muslims as the final word of God and *the* direction for humankind, touched these women as if it were a call to the faithful to come and submit themselves to that which is holy and divine. They responded with zeal and passion to Islamic scripture.

Finding Answers in Islam

Some of the women tried to prove Christianity to their Muslim husbands. They sought help from Christian leaders but were frustrated in their attempts. Some of the women struggled with letting go of Christianity even though they felt "Muslim." Several religious questions seemed unsettling to them. Whereas Islam tends to "have the answers," there is often confusion in Christian theology. In Islam there is only one God so how can Jesus also be God, the Muslims ask.

The Bible, viewed by many Christians as being the literal word of God, is also questioned. Muslims emphasize the many changes made over the centuries in the numerous manuscripts that make up the Bible and that it was written by those who only "felt inspired," often many years after the events occurred. They point out what they feel are contradictions in the Bible.

Muslims are well-versed in their beliefs and are often able to fill in the gaps for the confused person longing for God, for answers, for what to do to be at peace. Varying degrees of dissatisfaction with Christian theology as they perceive it is apparent in many of these women's stories. Some of the problems center in the concepts of Trinity, original sin, or Jesus as the Son of God or Jesus as God. Their frustration with some of these ideas helped to open the door for a "new" religious expression. . . .

And so began the faith journey for these women that would affect those around them—the families in which they were raised, their friends, their colleagues at work or school. Most of all, it would change the direction and flow of their own lives, not just in a religious sense but in every facet of their existence.

GLOSSARY

Allah: God.

burka (sometimes **burqa**): A long veil that covers the body except for the eyes and the fingertips, traditionally worn by Muslim women.

eid: Holy days in the Muslim calendar; the two most significant are the Eid al-Adha and the Eid al-Fitr.

Eid al-Adha: The annual feast day of sacrifice held on the tenth day of the Islamic month Dhu al-Hijjah, the month of pilgrimage.

Eid al-Fitr: The annual festival that celebrates the end of the month of fasting, Ramadan.

fatwa: An interpretation of Islamic religious law issued by an authoritative scholar or leader.

hajj: A pilgrimage, specifically to Mecca.

halal: Food that is properly prepared for Muslims in accordance with Koranic regulations.

hijab: A veil or head covering worn by some Muslim women.

imam: The leader of a session of prayer or a religious teacher; religious or political leader of a community.

Islam: Submission to God and to God's message revealed to Muhammad; the religion of Muslims.

jihad: Literally, a struggle; can refer to any struggle, from a personal striving to fulfill religious responsibilities to a holy war undertaken for the defense of Islam.

Koran (sometimes **Quran**): Literally, "the recitation"; the holy book of the Islamic faith, containing the revelations and prophecies of Muhammad.

Mecca: The holiest city in Islam, located in northwest Saudi Arabia.

minaret: A tower that is usually a component of a mosque, from which the call to prayer is given; a distinctive architectural symbol of Islam.

mosque: The Muslim building for worship and prayer.

muezzin: The individual who makes the call to prayer five times daily from the minaret of a mosque; used generally as a call to prayer.

Muhammad (sometimes **Mohammad**): The Prophet; founder of Islam, born in Mecca around A.D. 570.

Muslim (sometimes **Moslem**): A person who follows the Islamic faith, encompassing the teachings of Muhammad.

148

al Qaeda: The international terrorist organization chiefly sponsored by fundamentalist Muslim Osama bin Laden; believed to be responsible for executing the September 11, 2001, terrorist attacks against the United States.

Ramadan: The ninth month of the Muslim calendar, a month of fasting; the month in which the Koran is said to have been revealed to Muhammad.

sharia (sometimes **shariah**): The system of law in Islam based on the Koran.

Shia: One of the two major sects of Islam. See **Sunni.**

Sunni: One of the two major sects of Islam. See **Shia.**

ORGANIZATIONS TO CONTACT

The editors have compiled the following list of organizations concerned with the issues debated in this book. Descriptions are derived from materials provided by the organizations. All have publications or information available for interested readers. The list was compiled on the date of publication of the present volume; names, addresses, phone and fax numbers, and e-mail/Internet addresses may change. Be aware that many organizations take several weeks or longer to respond to inquiries, so allow as much time as possible.

American-Arab Anti-Discrimination Committee (ADC)
4201 Connecticut Ave. NW, Suite 300, Washington, DC 20008
(202) 244-2990 • fax: (202) 244-3196
e-mail: president@adc.org • Web site: www.adc.org
The ADC is committed to empowering Arab Americans, irrespective of religion. The committee aims to defend the civil rights of all people of Arab heritage in the United States, promote civic participation, encourage a balanced U.S. foreign policy in the Middle East, and support freedom and development in the Arab world.

American Moslem Foundation (AMF)
15004 SE 256th St., Covington, WA 98042
(253) 638-9989 • fax: (253) 588-8787
e-mail: amf@americanmoslemfdtn.org
Web site: www.americanmoslemfdtn.org
The AMF, a nonprofit charitable organization, assists American Muslims, recent immigrants, and their children in achieving "a balanced lifestyle" in their adopted homeland. The foundation also works to preserve their cultural and religious heritage, create a sense of community within this diverse group, and educate American citizens about Islam.

American Muslim Alliance
39675 Cedar Blvd., Suite 220E, Newark, CA 94560
(510) 252-9858 • fax: (510) 252-9863
e-mail: ama@amaweb.org • Web site: www.amaweb.org
The alliance strives for the political empowerment of the American Muslim community. The main goal of the alliance is to organize the American Muslim community into mainstream public affairs, civic discourse, and party politics across the United States.

Council of Islamic Schools in North America (CISNA)
1212 New York Ave. NW, Suite 450, Washington, DC 20005
(202) 789-2262 • fax: (202) 789-2550
e-mail: cisna@amconline.org • Web site: www.posttool.com/cisna/index.html
The CISNA is dedicated to the accreditation process as a responsible way of promoting excellence in Islamic schools. In consultation with Islamic schools in North America, CISNA has established structures, programs, and results for Islamic schools.

Council on American-Islamic Relations (CAIR)
453 New Jersey Ave. SE, Washington, DC 20003-4034
(202) 488-8787 • fax: (202) 488-0833
e-mail: cair@cair-net.org • Web site: www.cair-net.org

The CAIR was established to promote a positive image of Islam and Muslims in America. The group works to present an Islamic perspective on issues of importance to the American public and to empower the Muslim community in America through political and social activism.

Dar al Islam
PO Box 180, Abiquiu, NM 87510
(505) 685-4515
e-mail: drmshafi@msn.com • Web site: www.daralislam.org

Dar al Islam is a nonprofit educational organization founded in 1979 to transmit accurate and authentic knowledge of Islam in America. The group seeks to achieve its purpose through education in the broadest sense, through cooperation and networking, and through programs that benefit both Muslims and non-Muslims of North America.

Institute of Islamic Information and Education
PO Box 41129, Chicago, IL 60641-0129
(773) 777-7443 • fax: (773) 777-7199
e-mail: light@iiie.net • Web site: www.iiie.net

The institute is dedicated to the cause of Islam in North America and strives to elevate the image of Islam and Muslims by providing information about Islamic beliefs, history, and civilization from authentic sources.

International Institute of Islamic Thought
500 Grove St., Herndon, VA 20170
(703) 471-1133 • fax: (703) 471-3922
Web site: www.softechww.com/iiit

Concerned with general issues of Islamic thought, the institute works from an Islamic perspective to support research projects, organize intellectual and cultural meetings, and publish scholarly works.

Islamic Information Center of America
PO Box 4052, Des Plaines, IL 60016
(847) 541-8141 • fax: (847) 824-8436
e-mail: president@iica.org • Web site: www.iica.org/iica

The Islamic Information Center of America provides information about Islam to non-Muslims. The group operates a speakers' bureau and conducts its own research.

Islamic Society of North America (ISNA)
PO Box 38, Plainfield, IN 46168
(317) 839-8157 • fax: (317) 839-1840
e-mail: president@isna.net • Web site: www.isna.net

The ISNA works to advance the cause of Islam and Muslims in North America. ISNA activities include support for better schools, stronger outreach programs, organized community centers, and other Islamic programs. ISNA fosters unity among Muslims, which it sees as vital to an Islamic way of life, and publishes the magazine *Islamic Horizons*.

Islamic Supreme Council of America (ISCA)
1400 Sixteenth St. NW, Suite B112, Washington, DC 20036
(202) 939-3400 • fax: (202) 939-3410
e-mail: staff@islamicsupremecouncil.org
Web site: www.islamicsupremecouncil.org

The ISCA aims to provide practical solutions for American Muslims, based on the traditional Islamic legal rulings of an international advisory board. The group works to integrate traditional scholarship into the resolution of contemporary issues affecting Islamic beliefs in a modern, secular society.

Minaret of Freedom Institute
4323 Rosedale Ave., Bethesda, MD 20814
e-mail: mfi@minaret.org • Web site: www.minaret.org

The institute works to educate Muslims on the importance of liberty and free markets to a good society, while educating non-Muslims about the beliefs and contributions of Islam and the political realities of conflict between the two cultures.

Muslim Public Affairs Council
3010 Wilshire Blvd., Suite 217, Los Angeles, CA 90010
(213) 383-3443 • fax: (213) 383-9674
e-mail: salam@mpac.org • Web site: www.mpac.org

The council is a lobbying organization that works to establish a vibrant American Muslim community that will enrich American society by promoting Islamic values.

Muslim Students Association of the United States and Canada
PO Box 18612, Washington, DC 20036
(703) 820-7900 • fax: (703) 820-7888
e-mail: office@msa-national.org • Web site: www.msa-natl.org

The association is a student movement working to help Muslim student organizations implement Islamic programs and projects, mobilize and coordinate the human and material resources of Muslim student organizations, and educate, mobilize, and empower Muslim students.

Muslim Women's League (MWL)
3010 Wilshire Blvd., Suite 519, Los Angeles, CA 90010
(626) 358-0335
e-mail: mwl@mwlusa.org • Web site: www.mwlusa.org

MWL is a nonprofit American Muslim organization working to implement the values of Islam and thereby reclaim the status of women as free, equal, and vital contributors to society.

Nation of Islam (NOI)
7351 S. Stoney Island Ave., Chicago, IL 60649
(773) 324-6000
e-mail: email@noi.org • Web site: www.noi.org

The NOI represents followers of the Black Muslim movement in America, though the organization now eschews the use of the name *Black Muslim*. In addition to Islamic teachings, NOI specifically seeks social and economic equality and justice for African Americans.

BIBLIOGRAPHY

Books

Karen Armstrong	*Muhammad: A Biography of the Prophet.* San Francisco: HarperSanFrancisco, 1993.
Paul Findley	*Silent No More: Confronting America's False Images of Islam.* Beltsville, MD: Amana, 2001.
Fawaz Gerges	*America and Political Islam: Clash of Cultures or Clash of Interests?* New York: Cambridge University Press, 1999.
Yvonne Haddad	*The Muslims of America.* New York: Oxford University Press, 1991.
Yvonne Haddad and John L. Esposito, eds.	*Muslims on the Americanization Path?* New York: Oxford University Press, 2000.
Asma Gull Hasan	*Why I Am a Muslim: An American Odyssey.* London: Element, 2004.
Gilles Kepel	*Allah in the West: Islamic Movements in America and Europe.* Stanford, CA: Stanford University Press, 1997.
M.A. Muqtedar Khan	*American Muslims: Bridging Faith and Freedom.* Beltsville, MD: Amana, 2002.
Jeffery B. Lang	*Struggling to Surrender: Some Impressions of an American Convert to Islam.* Beltsville, MD: Amana, 2000.
Mohammad Nimer	*The North American Muslim Resource Guide: Muslim Community Life in the United States and Canada.* New York: Routledge, 2002.
Maryam Qudrat	*Torn Between Two Cultures: An Afghan-American Woman Speaks Out.* Sterling, VA: Capital, 2003.
Jane I. Smith	*Islam in America.* New York: Columbia University Press, 1999.
David Waines	*An Introduction to Islam.* New York: Cambridge University Press, 1995.
Vibert L. White Jr.	*Inside the Nation of Islam: A Historical and Personal Testimony by a Black Muslim.* Gainesville: University Press of Florida, 2001.
Michael Wolfe, ed.	*Taking Back Islam: American Muslims Reclaim Their Faith.* Emmaus, PA: Rodale Press, 2002.

Periodicals

Geneive Abdo	"Study Gauges 9/11 Effect on U.S. Muslims; Interest in Religion, Politics Deepens," *Chicago Tribune*, April 6, 2004.
Cathy Armer	"Islam in America: Lessons in Diversity," *Harvard University Gazette*, March 15, 2001.

Tara Bahrampour   "For Young Muslim Women, Coming of Age in New York Is a Complex Journey," *New York Times*, December 12, 1999.

Paul M. Barrett   "Spiritual Journey: One Imam Traces the Path of Islam in Black America," *Wall Street Journal*, October 24, 2003.

Larry Copeland   "War Is a Conflict for America's Muslim Teen," *USA Today*, November 7, 2001.

Peggy Goetz   "Being Muslim in America," *Orange County Register*, January 29, 2004.

Laurie Goodstein   "Influential American Muslims Temper Their Tone," *New York Times*, October 19, 2001.

Cathy Lynn Grossman   "Community Now 'Coming into Its Own'; Mosques Much More than Center of Religion," *USA Today*, April 26, 2001.

Salina Khan   "Employers Adjust to Muslim Customs; Ignorance, Not Prejudice, Cited in Cases," *USA Today*, June 25, 1999.

Don Lattin   "A Call for Muslim Pride After a Difficult Year," *San Francisco Chronicle*, August 31, 2002.

John Leo   "Pushing the Bias Button," *U.S. News & World Report*, June 9, 2003.

Waveney Ann Moore   "Striving to Bring Their Faith into Focus," *St. Petersburg Times*, September 11, 2003.

Caryle Murphy   "For Muslims, Benevolence Is Prevailing over Backlash," *Washington Post*, October 6, 2001.

Ahmed Nassef   "Tailor Muslim Practices to Fit Life in America," *Christian Science Monitor*, August 4, 2003.

Patrick O'Driscoll   "Muslims in the USA Live with New Fears After Attacks; Arab-Americans and Those Who Look Like Them Deal with Threats, Hate Crimes," *USA Today*, September 20, 2001.

Daniel Pipes and Khalid Duran   "Faces of American Islam," *Policy Review*, August/ September 2002.

John C. Raines   "The Politics of Religious Correctness: Islam and the West," *Cross Currents*, Spring 1996.

Imam Zaid Shakir   "American Muslims and a Meaningful Human Rights Discourse in the Aftermath of September 11, 2001," *Cross Currents*, Winter 2003.

Jeffery L. Sheler and Michael Betzold   "Muslim in America," *U.S. News & World Report*, October 29, 2001.

David Van Biema   "As American as . . . ; Although Scapegoated, Muslims, Sikhs, and Arabs Are Patriotic, Integrated—and Growing," *Time*, October 1, 2001.

Teresa Watanabe   "Frustrated U.S. Muslims Feel Marginalized Again," *Los Angeles Times*, September 27, 2002.

Jodi Wilgoren   "On Campus and on Knees, Facing Mecca," *New York Times*, February 13, 2001.

INDEX